Bernard Christian Steiner

History of Slavery in Connecticut

Bernard Christian Steiner

History of Slavery in Connecticut

ISBN/EAN: 9783743321625

Manufactured in Europe, USA, Canada, Australia, Japa

Cover: Foto ©ninafisch / pixelio.de

Manufactured and distributed by brebook publishing software (www.brebook.com)

Bernard Christian Steiner

History of Slavery in Connecticut

JOHNS HOPKINS UNIVERSITY STUDIES

IN

ICAL AND POLITICAL SCIENCE

HERBERT B. ADAMS, Editor

History is past Politics and Politics present History.—*Freeman*

ELEVENTH SERIES

IX-X

HISTORY OF SLAVERY IN CONNECTICUT

BY

BERNARD C. STEINER, PH. D.

BALTIMORE
THE JOHNS HOPKINS PRESS
PUBLISHED MONTHLY
September-October, 1893

CONTENTS.

	PAGE
INTRODUCTION	7
PERIOD I.—1636-1774.—Indian Slavery	9
Colonial Legislation on Slavery	11
Trials Concerning Slaves in Colonial Days	17
Social Condition of Slaves in Colonial Times	20
PERIOD II.—1774-1869.—Slaves in the Revolution	24
Opinions of the Forefathers on Slavery	28
State Legislation on Slavery	30
Cases Adjudicated in the Higher Courts with Reference to Slavery	37
Miss Prudence Crandall and her School	45
Nancy Jackson vs. Bulloch	52
The Negroes on the "Amistad"	56
Growth of the Anti-Slavery Spirit	68
Social Condition of Slaves	78
Appendix	83

HISTORY OF SLAVERY IN CONNECTICUT.

INTRODUCTION.

Few questions have been more interesting to the American people than slavery, and the number of works which have appeared upon the subject has been proportional to the interest aroused. The slavery of negroes has been discussed from almost every point of view, and yet the influence of slavery upon individual States of the Union and its different history and characteristics in the several States have not received the attention they deserve. There have been two able works dealing with this branch of the subject, tracing thoroughly the course of the institution of slavery in the two States of Massachusetts and Maryland.[1] As Massachusetts was the first State of the original number to free her slaves, and as Maryland was a typical Border State, these monographs, apart from their accuracy and completeness, have been valuable contributions to the study of slavery in the separate States, but they stand almost alone.

It has been the intention of the writer to take up the history of slavery in his native State—Connecticut. The development of slavery and the conditions surrounding it there were not greatly different from those existing in the larger State immediately to the north, yet there were certain phases of the "peculiar institution" in Connecticut which yield a

---

[1] I allude to Dr. Geo. Moore's "Notes on Slavery in Massachusetts" and Dr. J. R. Brackett's "Negro in Maryland." Tremain's "Slavery in the District of Columbia," in Univ. of Neb. Studies, and Ingle's "Negro in the District of Columbia." in J. H. U. Studies, are noteworthy. See also Morgan's brief account of "Slavery in New York" in the Am. Hist. Ass. Papers. I might add Ed. Bettle, "Notices of Negro Slavery as Connected with Pennsylvania," Vol. I., p. 365 ff., Penn. Hist. Soc. Memoirs.

noteworthy return to the student.[1] Though the formal abolition of slavery in Connecticut did not take place until 1848, there had been practically very few slaves in the State since 1800, and the treatment of the slave had been always comparatively mild and lenient. In the history of the opinion of the people in regard to slavery, we shall find two fairly well marked-off periods, under each of which we shall treat separately the legal, political, and social aspects of slavery. The first of these periods extends from the settlement of the colony until the passage of the Non-importation Act of 1774, and is characterized by a general acquiescence in the existence of slavery and a somewhat harsh slave code.

The second period, extending from 1774 to 1861, is marked by the diminution and extinction of slavery. It might be divided into two subdivisions. The first subdivision extends from October, 1774, to the rise of the Abolitionists, about 1830, and is characterized by the gradual emancipation of the slaves and amelioration of their condition.

In the second subdivision, lasting from about 1830 till the Civil War, we find the formal abolition of slavery and the rise of the slavery question as a political issue, culminating in the resistance to the Fugitive Slave Act, and ending in the Act of 1857. The period closes with the acceptance of the Fifteenth Amendment in 1869.

---

[1] The author regrets that he was unable to consult Dr. Wm. C. Fowler's "Historical Status of the Negro in Connecticut" until these pages were passing through the press. Any new matter therein contained has been embodied in foot-notes, as far as possible. The labor and research Dr. Fowler bestowed on his paper make it very valuable. It appeared in Dawson's Historical Magazine for 1874, Vol. XXIII., pp. 12-18, 81-85, 148-153, 260-266.

PERIOD I.—1636-1774.

INDIAN SLAVERY.

In Connecticut, as in many other States, the first slaves were not of African race, but were aborigines, taken in battle and sold as slaves, in the same manner as the Anglo-Saxon forefathers of the early settlers had-sold the captives of their spear, over a millennium before. After the fierce and bloody Pequod War, the colonists found on their hands a number of captive Indians, whose disposition formed a pressing question. It did not take long to decide it. To the shame of the conquerors, " Ye prisoners were devided, some to those of the River [Connecticut] and the rest to us" of Massachusetts.[1] Of those taken by the latter, they sent "the male children to Bermudas, by Mr. William Pierce, and the women and maid children are disposed about in the towns. There have now been slain and taken, in all, about 700." Connecticut's disposition of her share was, doubtless, much the same as that described above. In the same spirit, the Articles of Confederation of the United New England Colonies, in which both Connecticut and New Haven were included, when drawn up on May 19, 1643, provided that "the whole advantage of the warr (if it please God to bless their Endeavours), whether it be in lands, goods, or *persons*, shall be proportionally divided among the said Confederates."[2]

The Articles of Confederation also provided "that, if any servant run away from his master into any of these confederated jurisdictions, that, in such case, upon certificate of one magistrate in the jurisdiction of which the said servant fled, or upon other due proof, the said servant shall be delivered, either to his master or any other, that pursues and brings such certificate or proof." This was the first fugitive slave law in force in Connecticut.

---

[1] Mass. Hist. Soc. Coll., Series IV., Vol. III., p. 360.
[2] Plymouth Col. Rec., Vol. IX., p. 4.

Since it was found that certain Indian villages harbored fugitive Indians, the Confederation, on Sept. 5, 1646, decided that such villages might be raided and the inhabitants carried off, women and children being spared as much as possible, and added, to its eternal shame, that "because it will be chargeable keeping Indians in prison and, if they should escape, they are liable to prove more insolent and dangerous after, it was thought fit that upon such seizure...the magistrates of the jurisdiction deliver up the Indians seized to the party or parties endamaged, either to serve or to be shipped out and exchanged for negroes, as the cause will justly bear."[1] The Connecticut Code of 1646, following this resolve in its language, recognizes Indian and negro slavery.[2]

The Confederation, in 1646, took active part in endeavoring to make Gov. Kieft of New Netherlands return "an Indian captive liable to publicke punishment fled from her master at Hartford" and "entertained in your house at Hartford and, though required by the magistrate," she was "under the hands of your agent there denyed, and was said to have been either marryed or abused by one of your men." " Such a servant," they say, "is parte of her master's estate and a more considerable part than a beast; our children will not longe be secure if this be suffered." This last sentence clearly shows the outcropping of the patriarchal idea. Kieft refused to give her up, and said, "as concerns the Barbarian handmade," it is "apprehended by some, that she is no slave, but a freewoman, because she was neither taken in war, nor bought with price, but was in former time placed with me by her parents for education."[3] By the Inter-Colonial Treaty of Sept. 19, 1650, the provision of the Articles of Confederation, in regard to fugitives, was extended to include the intercourse of the New Englanders and the Dutch.[4] King Philip's War again threw many Indian captives into the settlers' hands and,

---

[1] Hazard, II., p. 63.
[2] Title " Indians," Conn. Rec., I., 531. Not in Revision of 1715. Plymouth Records, IX., 6, 64, 190.
[4] Hurd, " Law of Freedom and Bondage in the U. S.," I., 269.

on May 10, 1677,[1] the General Court decreed, "for the prevention of those Indians running away, that are disposed in service by the Authority, that are of the enemie and have submitted to mercy, such Indians, if they be taken, shall be in the power of his master to dispose of him, as a captive by transportation out of the country." The syntax of the enactment is confused, its cruelty is clear.

The number of Indian slaves seems to have gradually decreased from death, intermarriage with negroes, and emancipation, though as late as May 1, 1690, Gov. Leisler of New York met with the Commissioners of Massachusetts, Plymouth, and Connecticut, and they all covenanted that in the contemplated Indian war, "all plunder and captives (if any happen) shall be divided to the officers and soldiers, according to the custom of War."[2]

Though the colonists entertained no doubt of their right to sell Indian captives, better Puritan nature revolted against the idea of perpetual hereditary slavery, and, as early as 1722, we find doubts expressed as to the status of the child of an Indian slave.[3]

Dr. Fowler states that Indian slaves were not considered as valuable as negroes.

Further remarks as to legislation in regard to Indian slaves will be found in a subsequent section.

COLONIAL LEGISLATION ON SLAVERY.

The earliest law on any of Connecticut's statute-books in regard to slavery is a quotation from Exodus xxi. 16, placed tenth among the Capital Laws of Connecticut, on Dec. 1, 1642, "If any man stealeth a man or mankind, he shall be put to death." This, however, was understood, of course, only to include in its protection persons of white race.

When or how negro slavery was introduced into Connecticut, we have no records to show. "It was never directly

---

[1] Conn. Col. Rec., II., 308.
[2] N. Y. Doc. Hist., II., pp. 134, 157.
[3] Trumbull's "Connecticut," Vol. I., p. 417. Fowler, p. 152.

established by statute," says the editor of the Revision of the State's Laws in 1821,¹ "but has been indirectly sanctioned by various statutes and frequently recognized by courts, so that it may be said to have been established by law."² Few slaves were imported at first, and, on May 17, 1660, we find the first reference to negroes in the Connecticut Records."³ Then the distrust of bondmen and the fear of treachery in slaves, nearly always shown by masters, is revealed in the General Court's order " that neither Indian nor negar servants shall be required to train, watch, or ward in the Colony."⁴

The number of negroes was "few," not above thirty, only two of whom were christened, in 1680,⁵ and not until ten years later had they sufficiently increased so as to call the attention of the legislators to their regulation. Connecticut began her black code in October, 1690,⁶ by passing several measures, providing that a "negro, mulatto, or Indian servant" found wandering out of the bounds of the town to which he belonged, without a ticket or pass from an Assistant, or Justice of the Peace, or his owner, shall be accounted a runaway and may be seized by any one finding him, brought before the next authority and returned to his master, who must pay the charges. Even a ferryman, transporting a slave without a pass, was liable to a penalty of twenty shillings for each offense.⁷ A free negro without a pass must pay the costs if stopped and brought before a magistrate.

The last two laws were repealed in October. 1797.⁸

The next statute, save one, referring to slaves was passed

---

¹ Probably Swift, author of the well-known "System."
² Revision of 1821, Title 93, Sec. 7, note.
³ Dr. Fowler ("Hist. Status," p. 12) says negro slaves were in New Haven Colony in 1644.
⁴ Conn. Col. Rec., 1., 349.
⁵ They came sometimes three and four a year from Barbadoes. Conn. Col. Rec., III., p. 298. Answer to Queries.
⁶ Conn. Col. Rec., IV., p. 40. Revision of 1808. Title CL., Ch. I., Secs. 1-4.
⁷ This amount was later changed to $3.34.
⁸ Hurd. II., p. 42.

in 1703.[1] This shows clearly the survival in colonial days of the *potestas* of the *pater familias* coming down from the absolute dominion of the house-father in ancient times. It prohibits any "licensed innkeeper, victualler, taverner, or retailer of strong drink" from "suffering any one's sons, apprentices, servants, or negroes to sit drinking in his house, or have any manner of drink there, without special order from parents or masters."

Slaves seem now, for some time, to be repressed by laws continually growing harsher. In May, 1708,[2] the General Court, taking into consideration that "divers rude and evil-minded persons, for the sake of filthy lucre, do receive property stolen by slaves," and desiring to prevent this and to better govern the slaves, decreed that any one buying or receiving from slaves property without an order from their masters, must return the property and double its value in addition, or, if he has disposed of the original property, treble its value, and, if he will not do this, he is to be whipped with not over twenty stripes. The slaves caught in theft were to be whipped with not over thirty stripes, whether the receivers of the goods from them were found or not. Further, "whereas negro and mulatto servants or slaves[3] are become numerous in some parts of this Colonie and are very apt to be turbulent and often quarrelling with white people to the great disturbance of the peace," it is enacted that a negro disturbing the peace or offering to strike a white person, is to be subject to a penalty of not over thirty stripes.

In spite of these harsher laws, emancipation was becoming somewhat common, and the Colony feared that it would have to support negroes whose years of usefulness had been spent in work for their masters, and who were manumitted by them.

---

[1] Conn. Col. Rec., IV., 438. A penalty of 10 shillings was to be imposed for a breach of this act. It does not seem to have been included in any of the revisions of the statutes.

[2] Conn. Col. Rec., V., p. 52. This was in force in 1808. Title CL., Ch. I., Sec. 5.

[3] Revision of 1750, p. 229.

when old and helpless. To prevent this, in May, 1702,[1] the legislature provided that slaves, set free and coming to want, must be relieved by the owners, their heirs, executors, or administrators. To this act a second one was added in 1711, providing that if the owners or their representatives refused to maintain such emancipated slaves, it should be the duty of the selectmen of the various towns to do so, and then to sue the owners, or their representatives, for the expense[2] incurred.

The terrible war between the South Carolinians and the Tuscaroras, ending with the overthrow of the latter, left a large number of Indian prisoners in the hands of the Carolinians, who shipped them as slaves to the other colonies. This importation of vengeful, warlike savages alarmed the people of Connecticut and led to the first steps towards prohibition of the slave trade. The Governor and Council met on July 8, 1715, and considering the fact that several have brought into the colony Carolina Indians, "which have committed many cruel and bloody outrages" there, and may draw off "our Indians," if their importation be continued, and so "much mischief" may follow, they decided to prohibit importation of Indian slaves, until the meeting of the Assembly, and to require each ship entering port with Indians on board to give bond of £50 to transport them from the colony in twenty days. Further, Indians brought into the colony hereafter are to be "kept in strictest custody," confined and "prevented from communicating with other Indians," unless owner give the same bond as above to remove them from Connecticut in twenty days.[3]

The next October, the General Court, copying a Massachusetts Act of 1712, made the prohibition of bringing in Indian slaves permanent, since "divers conspiracies, outrages, barbarities, murders, burglaries, thefts, and other no-

---

[1] Conn. Col. Rec., IV., 375. A similar act to the same purpose was passed in May, 1703. Conn. Col. Rec., IV., 408. See p. 32.

[2] Conn. Col. Rec., V., 233. The whole was in the revision of 1808, Title CL., Ch. I., Sec. 11.

[3] Conn. Col. Rec., V., 516.

torious crimes at sundry times and, especially of late, have been perpetrated by Indians and other slaves,...being of a malicious and vengeful spirit, rude and insolent in their behaviour, and very ungovernable, the overgreat number of which, considering the different circumstances in this Colony from the plantations in the islands and our having considerable numbers of Indians, natives of our country,...may be of pernicious consequence."[1] The legislature decreed the forfeiture of all Indians hereafter imported, and the payment of a fine of £50 by shipmaster or other persons bringing Indians.

The preamble quoted above shows that this measure was not prompted by affection for the slaves, but by fear of them; but it was the beginning of the end—the first law restricting slaveholders' rights in Connecticut, to be followed by one and another of the same restrictive kind, until all men who trod the soil of the State were free.

The next law on the records was passed in May, 1723, and provided that a slave out of doors after 9 P. M., without order from master or mistress, might be secured and brought before a Justice of the Peace by any citizen and, if found guilty, should receive not over ten stripes, unless the master were willing to pay a fine of ten shillings[2] to release him. Any one who should receive such a slave must, on conviction, pay a like fine, half to the town and half to the informer.

The black code was completed by the act of May, 1730, declaring that a slave speaking such words as would be actionable in a free person, should be whipped, on conviction, with not over forty stripes and sold for the costs, unless the master were willing to pay them. However, there was a ray of justice in the provision of the law that the slave might make the same pleas and offer the same evidence as a free person.[3]

---

[1] Conn. Col. Rec., V., 534. Fee of 2s. 6d. for registering slave, which must be done in twenty-four hours after arrival. The slave must be taken away within a month.
[2] Amount to be paid later changed to $1.67. Conn. Col. Rec., VI., 391. Repealed by Ch. IV., Oct. 1797.
[3] Conn. Col. Rec. VII., 290. In Revision of 1750. p. 40.

From this time on, the more engrossing subjects of the struggle between the French and the colonists, and the growth of material prosperity seem to have thrust aside the topic of slavery from the legislative halls. For forty-four years we find few more laws.[1] It is true, however, that at the General Assembly in 1738, "it was inquired—whether the infant slaves of Christian masters may be baptized in the right of their masters, they solemnly promising to train them in the knowledge and admonition of the Lord; and whether it is the duty of such masters to offer such children and thus religiously to promise." To the great credit of the colonists, both these questions were answered affirmatively, and thus the devout Christians of Connecticut, preserving the solidarity of the family, unconsciously went back to the early Aryan custom, that the God of the house-father should be worshiped by all under his sway. The growth of free ideas,[2] the coming of the Revolution, the increase of the slaves, "injurious," it was thought, to the poor and "inconvenient"—for the best motives are apt to be mixed of good and evil—led, in October. 1774, to the enactment of the law that "no Indian, negro, or mulatto slave shall at any time hereafter[3] be brought or imported into this State,[4] by sea or land, from any place or places whatsoever, to be disposed of, left, or sold within the State," and any offender against this law should pay £100.[5] So the State set herself as resolutely against the slave trade, as she was destined to do later against slavery itself.

---

[1] In 1727 it was enacted that masters and mistresses of Indian children were to use their utmost endeavors to teach them to read English, and to instruct them in the Christian faith. Reprint of 1737, p. 339. Hurd, I., p. 272.

[2] Conn. Col. Rec., XIV., 155. May, 1773, "Negro's memorial postponed to October." Nothing more of it.

[3] Conn. Col. Rec., XIV., 329.

[4] Note the early use of the word.

[5] Later the sum was fixed at $334. By act of October, 1798, such prosecutions must be begun in three years. Revision of 1808, Title CI., Ch. III. By Revision of 1821, Title 93, Sec. 5, fine put at $350.

A good review of the legal condition of the slave in these days is given by Judge Reeves,[1] who, "lest the slavery, which prevailed in this State, be forgotten," mentioned "some things that show that slavery here was very far from being of the absolute rigid kind. The master had no control over the life of his slave. If he killed him, he was liable to the same punishment, as if he killed a freeman. The master was as liable to be sued by the slave, in an action for beating, and wounding, or for immoderate chastisement, as he would be if he had thus treated an apprentice. A slave was capable of holding property in character of devisee or legatee. If the master should take away such property, his slave would be entitled to an action against him by his *prochein ami*. From the whole, we see that slaves had the same right of life and property as apprentices, and that the difference betwixt them was this, an apprentice is a servant for time and the slave is a servant for life."[2]

TRIALS CONCERNING SLAVES IN COLONIAL DAYS.

I have been able to obtain but few recorded cases in which the question of freedom or slavery came up in the courts

---

[1] Law of Baron and Femme, pp. 340-1. Reeves says, "If a slave married a free woman, with the consent of his master, he was emancipated; for his master had suffered him to contract a relation inconsistent with a state of slavery." Dane's Abridgment. II., p. 313, says, "In Connecticut the slave was, by statute, specially forbidden to contract." *Vide* Hurd, II., p. 42.

[2] In the Code of 1650, under the title, "Masters, Sojourners, Servants," the last named are forbidden, under penalty, to trade without permission of their masters, and provision is made for their recapture by public authority if they run away. Refractory servants are to be punished by extension of their time of service. The lawmakers, probably, had in mind the class known as indented servants, or redemptioners, in formulating this act. (Conn. Rec., I., 539.) In the Revision of 1715, title "Debts," it was provided that a debtor without estate " shall satisfy the debt by service, if the creditor shall require it, in which case he shall not be disposed in service to any but of the English nation," to prevent the sale of the debtor to the French in Canada. Delinquents under a penal law were, by an act of 1725, to be disposed of at service to any inhabitant of the Colony " to defray the Costs." (Reprint 1737, p. 314.)

during this first period. In the end of 1702 or beginning of 1703, a slave, Abda, belonging to Capt. Thomas Richards of Hartford, escaped from his master and was succored by Capt. Joseph Wadsworth of Hartford, who, on Feb. 12th, 1703, opposed the constable in executing a writ of arrest on Abda. This early fugitive slave case was brought before the Governor and Council on Feb. 25.¹ They recommended the County Court to examine the case. Apparently Abda brought an action on the case against Mr. Richards, as a counter suit, claiming damages of £20 from his master, " for his unjust holding and detaining the said Abda in his service as his bondsman, for the space of one year past." The verdict was for £12 damages, " thereby virtually establishing Abda's right to freedom," which he, a mulatto, seems to have claimed largely on account of his white blood.²

Mr. Richards pressed the case further and, in May, 1704, obtained from the General Court an order to have a hearing before it in October, on his petition concerning Abda.³ At that time the case was brought up and the fugitive was returned to his master, as Gov. Saltonstall said, " according to the laws and constant practice of this Colony and all other plantations (as well as by the civil law) such persons as are born of negro bondwomen are themselves in like condition, *i. e.* born in servitude.⁴ Nor can there be any precedent in this Government, or any of Her Majesty's plantations, produced to the contrary and, though the law of this Colony doth not say that such persons as are born of negro woman and supposed to be mulattoes shall be slaves (which was needless, because of the constant practice by which they are held as such), yet it saith expressly that no man shall put away or make free his negro or mulatto slave, etc., which

---

¹ Conn. Col. Rec., XV., 548.
² Moore's " Notes on Slavery," p. 112, quoting J. H. Trumbull in Conn. *Courant*, Nov. 9, 1850. Fowler, " Hist. Status," pp. 14-16.
³ Conn. Col. Rec., IV., 478. Papers in Miscellaneous, II., pp. 10-21.
⁴ This following as a precedent the Roman Law maxim, " Partus sequitur ventrem," at this early day in New England is noteworthy.

undeniably shows and declares an approbation of such servitude, and that mulattoes may be held as slaves within this government."[1]

A later fugitive slave[2] we find advertised for in the New York *Mercury* on July 28, 1760, and the advertisement has many little touches which go to show how slaves lived and were treated. "Run away from Abraham Davenport of Stamford in Conn., the 4th of June instant, a Mulatto Man Slave named Vanhall, aged 31 years, about 5 feet 4 or 5 inches high, very swarthy; has a small Head and Face, a large Mouth, and has an odd Action with his Head, when talking with any Person ; has very long Arms and large Hands for a Person of his size and has an old Countenance for one of his Age; his Hair, like others of his kind was but lately cut off; was brought up to the Farming business, is a lively active Fellow and pretends to understand the Violin. Had on, when he went away, a Felt Hat, a Grey Cut Wig, a light homespun Flannel lappelled Vest, which had been lined with fine old Cotton and Linnen Ticken, Doeskin Breeches, he took several pairs of Stockings and one or two pairs of Shoes, a Violin and a small Hatchet, &c., and 'tis probable he might change his Cloaths. Whoever takes up and secures said Mulatto, so that his Master may have him again, shall receive £5. Reward, and reasonable charges paid."

Late in Colonial times,[3] we find Hagar, a New London negress, appearing before the Governor and Council and pleading that she and her children were lawfully freed by her former master, James Rogers, and so her refusal to yield herself as a slave to James Rogers, Jr., his grandson, was justified. The decision was that she should give bond to prove her freedom at the next County Court and be secured from molestation in the meanwhile.

---

[1] Moore, Notes on Slavery. pp. 24-25, quoting J. H. Trumbull's "Hist. Notes," etc., No. VI.
[2] Am. Hist. Mag., XIII., p. 498. *Vide* Fowler, " Hist. Status," p. 148.
[3] Conn. Col. Rec., XV., p. 582.

SOCIAL CONDITION OF SLAVES IN COLONIAL TIMES.

On this topic comparatively little can be found. Each large[1] village had its negro corner in the Meeting House gallery and in the graveyard. In the larger towns, such as Norwich, New Haven, Hartford, and New London, there were several hundred negroes. They were for the most part indulgently treated and admitted, at least in many places, into the local churches as fellow-members with the white population.[2] They must, however, occupy their allotted gallery seats, which in Torrington were boarded up so that the negroes could see no one and be seen by none. If they attempted to sit elsewhere, or refused to go to church if made to sit there, excommunication was apt to follow.[3]

Among early negro slaves recorded in Connecticut are some belonging to John Pantry of Hartford in 1653, and one Cyrus, belonging to Henry Wolcott, Jr., of Windsor, and rated at £30 in his inventory.[4] Miss Caulkins states that early in the eighteenth century slaves were worth from 60 shillings to £30, and that later the best were valued as high as £100. She instances the purchase of a negro boy by Rev. William Hart of Saybrook in 1749 for £290, Old Tenor, about equal to £60 in coin.[5] In 1708, and probably the same state of things continued later, we learn the negroes mostly came from "neighboring governments, save some times half a dozen a year from the West Indies"; but "none ever imported by the Royal African Company or separate traders."[6]

---

[1] In 1726 Suffield voted Rev. Mr. Devotion £20 towards purchasing negroes. Trumbull's "Hartford County," II., p. 406.

[2] E. g. Phebe, colored servant of Joel Thrall, joined Torrington Church, 1756. Orcutt's "Torrington," p. 211.

[3] Jacob Prince, a free negro, was so excommunicated in Goshen. Orcutt's "Torrington," p. 218.

[4] 1680, slaves sold at £22. Conn. Col. Rec., III., 298.
Stiles, "Ancient Windsor," p. 489, notices an early deed of sale, dated 1694, from a Bostonian to a Windsor man, for a negro. Twenty-one negroes died in South Windsor from 1736 to 1768, of which number eleven belonged to the Wolcott family.

[5] Hist. of Norwich, p. 328. Vide Fowler, "Hist. Status," p. 148.

[6] Conn. Col. Rec., XV., 557.

For the most part, only one or two negroes were owned by any person. In some parts of the State, as at Waterbury,[1] we find it customary for the clergymen to have two slaves, a man and a woman. Occasionally, however, more were owned by a wealthy man, as in the case of Capt. John Perkins of Hanover Society,[2] Norwich, who left fifteen slaves by his will in 1761. The slaves were generally kindly treated and were docile, though we hear of the death of a man in 1773 from lockjaw, caused by a bite in the thumb by a young slave he was chastising.[3] The majority, however, could show much more amicable relations. For example, Mingo,[4] in Waterbury, who, about 1730, when a boy, was hired out by his master to drive a plow, later to work with a team and, 1764, at his master's death, was allowed to choose which son he would live with. He chose to live with the one who kept the old homestead and remained there until he began keeping a tavern, when he left and went to another son's. He had a family, and left considerable property at his death in 1800. Indeed, as early as 1707, we have evidence of the possession of property by a negro, for, in October of that year, Lieut. John Hawley, administrator to the estate of John Negro, was granted power by the General Court to sell £10 worth of his land, it appearing from the Fairfield County Probate Records that he owed that amount more than his moveables would pay.[5]

Towards the close of this period, the reasonableness and justice of holding slaves began to be questioned and eman-

---

[1] Bronson's "Waterbury," 321. [2] Caulkins' "Norwich," p. 328.
[3] Caulkins' "Norwich," p. 329. Godfrey Malbone of Brooklyn owned 50 or 60 slaves. Fowler, p. 16.
[4] The first negro there. Bronson's "Waterbury," p. 321. He also refers to Parson Scovil's Dick, brought from Africa when a boy and sold several times, with the understanding he could return when he pleased. He left some property at his death in 1835, aged 90. Also to I. Woodruff of Westbury, who owned an Indian woman till her death in 1774. In Wintonbury (Bloomfield) there were probably not over a dozen slaves in all in colonial times. In Bristol a few of the farms were cultivated by slave labor, and one family owned three negroes. Trumbull's "Hartford County," II., pp. 35, 51.
[5] Conn. Col. Rec., VI., 35.

cipations, "from a conscientious regard to justice," begin to appear. One man in Norwich not only freed three slaves, but, "as a compensation for their services, leased them a very valuable farm on very moderate rate."[1] That section of the State seems to have been considerably stirred on this question, and in the Norwich *Packet*, July 7, 1774, we find an anti-slavery appeal of sufficient vigor to warrant quotation in full:

"To all you who call yourselves Sons of Liberty in America, Greeting:

"My Friends, We know in some good measure the inestimable value of liberty, But were we once deprived of her she would then appear much more valuable than she now appears. We also see her, standing as it were, tiptoe on the highest bough ready for flight. Why is she departing? What is it disturbs her repose? Surely, some foul monster of hideous shape and hateful kind, opposite in its nature to hers, with all its frightful appearances and properties, iron hands and leaden feet, formed to gripe and crush, hath intruded itself into her peaceful habitation and ejected her. Surely this must be the case, for we know oppositions can not dwell together. Is it not time, high time to search for this Achan? this disturber of Israel? High time, I say, to examine for the cause of those dark and gloomy appearances that cast a shade over our glory, and is not this it? Are we not guilty of the same crime we impute to others? Of the same facts, that we say are unjust, cruel, arbitrary, despotic, and without law in others? Paul argued in this manner—'Thou that teachest another, teachest thou not thyself? Thou that preachest a man should not steal, dost thou steal? Thou that makest thy boast of the law, through breaking the law dishonorest thou God?' And may we not use the same mode of argument and say—We that declare, and that with much warmth and zeal, it is unjust, cruel, barbarous, unconstitutional, and without law to enslave, *do we enslave?* Yes, verily we do! *A black cloud witnesseth*

---

[1] Caulkins' "Norwich," p. 329.

against us and our own mouths condemn us! How preposterous our conduct! How vain and hypocritical our pretences! Can we expect to be free, so long as we are determined to enslave? (Signed) Honesty."[1]

Before we turn from Colonial times,[2] the fact is worthy of note that, though "redemptioners" were not common in Connecticut, white men were often bound out to service for a term of years, as in other colonies. We find in 1670 a man sold to the Barbadoes for four years as a slave, for "notorious stealing," "breaking up and robbing of" two mills and living "in a renegade manner in the wilderness." In 1756, a town pauper in Waterbury,[3] for stealing, was whipped and bound out to the plaintiff, as a servant, till the sum stolen and the costs be paid by his work, and the law on the statute-books was that "all single persons, who lived an idle and riotous life," might be bound out to service to pay the costs of prosecution.

---

[1] The emancipation of slaves is not looked on by Dr. Fowler as greatly contributing to their welfare. He quotes an essay published in 1793 by Noah Webster, Jr.: "Nor does the restoration to freedom correct the depravity of their hearts. Born and bred beneath the frowns of power, neglected and despised in youth, they abandon themselves to ill company and low vicious pleasures, till their habits are formed; when manumission, instead of destroying their habits and repressing their corrupt inclinations. serves to afford the more numerous opportunities of indulging both. Thus an act of strict justice to the slave. very often, renders him a more worthless member of society." "Hist. Status of the Negro." p. 149.

[2] Dr. Fowler; "Hist. Status." pp. 12-13, calls attention to the fact that Louis Berbice. from Dutch Guiana. killed by his master, Gysbert Opdyck, commissary at the Dutch fort in Hartford, in Nov., 1639, was probably the first negro in Conn. He gives a list of the early owners of negroes and notes that in 1717, the Lower House passed a bill prohibiting negroes purchasing land. or living in families of their own. without liberty from the town.

[3] Bronson's Waterbury. p. 321.

PERIOD II.—1774-1869.

SLAVES IN THE REVOLUTION.[1]

The subject of using negroes in the army first came before the General Assembly in May, 1777, when a committee was appointed "to take[2] into consideration the state and condition of the negro and mulatto slaves in this State, and what may be done for their emancipation." I would hazard a guess that this committee was appointed in consequence of a resolution of the town of Enfield, on March 31, 1777, appointing a committee of three to prefer a memorial to the Assembly, to "pray[3] that the Negroes in this State be released from their Slavery and Bondage." The Assembly's committee, of which Hon. Matthew Griswold was chairman, reported a recommendation that the effective negro and mulatto slaves be allowed to enlist with the Continental bat-

---

[1] CONNECTICUT COMMITTEE OF SAFETY.

Monday, September 4, 1775.

At a meeting of the committee On information, by letter, from Major Latimer, "that one of the Vessels lately taken by Captain *Wallace*, of the *Rose*, man-of-war, &c., at *Stonington*, was by stress of weather drove back to *New-London*, with one white man, a petty officer, and three negroes on board, and were in his custody, and asking directions how to dispose of them, &c. And by other information it appears that two of the negroes belong to Deputy Governour *Cooke*, of *Rhode-Island*, and were lately seized and robbed from him, with and on board a vessel, by said *Wallace*, and that the other belonged to one Captain *Collins*. And, on consideration,

Voted and Ordered, That the Major give information to the owner of the vessel, and, on his request, deliver her up to him, and send the white man to the jail at *Windham*, and the three negroes to the care of, and to be employed for the present by, Captain *Niles*, at *Norwich*, who is fixing out a small Armed Vessel, &c., until the Governour shall advise Deputy Governour *Cooke* of the matter, that they may, on proper notice, be returned to their owners."—Am. Arch., IV., III., p. 672.

[2] Livermore, "Historical Research," p. 113.

[3] Trumbull's "Hartford County," II., p. 151.

talions now raising in this State, under the following regulations and restrictions: viz., that all such negro and mulatto slaves as can procure, either by bounty, hire, or in any other way, such a sum to be paid to their masters, as such negro and mulatto shall be judged to be reasonably worth by the selectman of the town where such negro or mulatto belongs, shall be allowed to enlist into either of said battalions, and shall thereupon be, *de facto*, free and emancipated; and that the master of such negro or mulatto shall be exempted from the support and maintenance of such negro or mulatto, in case" he "shall hereafter become unable to support and maintain himself." Further, if a slave desire to enlist for the war, he may be appraised by the selectmen and his master may receive the bounty and half the slave's annual wages until the appraised sum be equaled. The Upper House rejected this report.

At that session, however, an act was passed that any two men, "who should procure an able bodied soldier," should be exempted from the draft, during the continuance of the substitute's enlistment. "Of recruits," writes Dr. J. H. Trumbull, "and draughted men thus furnished, neither the selectmen nor commanding officers questioned the color, or the civil status; white and black, bond and free, if able bodied, went on the roll together, accepted as the representatives or substitutes of their employers."

In October, 1777,[1] the Assembly passed an act similar to the one proposed in May. It authorized the selectmen, on application from a master of a slave, to inquire "into the age, abilities, circumstances, and character" of the slave, and, being satisfied "that it was likely to be consistent with his real advantage, and that it was probable that he would be able to support himself, and is of good and peaceable life and conversation," they could free the master from all liability for support of his freedman. This offered an additional inducement to masters to free slaves to make up the

---

[1] Revision of 1808, Title CL., Ch. I., Sec. 12. *Vide* Stiles' "Anc. Windsor," I., p. 491.

town's quota of men, and Dr. Trumbull says "some hundreds of black slaves and free men enlisted." The rolls of the companies show no distinction of color. The surnames Liberty, Freeman, Freedom are frequently found.[1] In Wethersfield, on the blank leaves of the book of town votes, among records of emancipation from motives of humanity, or for money, we find record of John Wright and Luke Fortune freeing their slave Abner Andrew, on May 20, 1777, to be their substitute in the army. Other certificates free slaves on condition of "enlisting in the Continental Army in Col. Wallis' Regiment" and "and after the customary three years service," and, as late as 1780, Caesar was manumitted by David Griswold there, on "condition of enlistment and faithfully serving out the time of enlistment," which was three years.[2]

David Humphreys commanded a company entirely composed of negroes, their roster showing fifty-six names,[3] first of which is Jack Arabas, of whom we shall hear again. It was said Humphreys nobly volunteered to command the company, when others refused, and continued its captain until peace was declared. The company was in Meigs' (later Butler's) regiment of the Connecticut Line.

At Fort Griswold, when Col. Ledyard was murdered, a negro soldier named Lambert avenged his death by thrusting a bayonet through the British officer who slew his superior, and then fell a martyr, pierced by thirty-three bayonet wounds.[4]

"As to the efficiency of the service they rendered," says Dr. J. H. Trumbull,[5] "I can say nothing from the records,

---

[1] Livermore's "Historical Research," p. 115.
[2] Am. Hist. Mag., XXI., 422. Trumbull's "Hartford County," II., 475.
[3] Williams' "Hist. of Negro Race in America," I., 361.
[4] Wilson, "Rise and Fall of the Slave Power," I., p. 19.
Livermore's "Historical Research," p. 115. Lib Quy, native African, was a trusty Continental soldier from Norwich in 1780 and '81 (Caulkins' "Norwich," p. 331). Oliver Mitchell, a negro Revolutionary soldier, died of a fit in his boat, March, 1840, in which he had been to Hartford to draw his pension (Stiles' "Ancient Windsor," I., p. 489).

save what is to be gleaned from scattered files.... So far as my acquaintance extends, almost every family has its traditions of the good and faithful service of a black servant or slave, who was killed in battle or served through the war and came home to tell stories of hard fighting and draw his pension. In my own town—not a large one—I remember five such pensioners, three of whom I believe had been slaves, and were in fact slaves to the day of their death; for (and this explains the uniform action of the General Assembly on petitions for emancipation) neither the towns nor the State were inclined to exonerate the master, at a time when slavery was becoming unprofitable, from the obligation to provide for the old age of his slave."

An interesting Revolutionary case is that of the slaves of Col. William Browne of Salem, Mass., a Tory, whose large farm in Lyme was confiscated. It was leased for a term of years with nine slaves, who petitioned for liberty in 1779, through Benjamin Huntington, administrator on confiscated estates. The lessee offered to consent to their freedom without requiring a diminution in the rent. Mr. Huntington drew up their petition to the Assembly,[1] stating that they, "all friends to America, but slaves lately belonging to Col. Wm. Browne," who "fled from his native country to his master, King George, where he now lives like a poor slave," "though they have flat noses, crooked shins, and other queerness of make, peculiar to Africans, are yet of the human race, free-born in our country, taken from thence by manstealers, and sold in this country, as cattle in the market, without the least act of our own to forfeit liberty; but we hope our good mistress, *the free State of Connecticut*, engaged in a war with tyranny, will not sell honest Whigs and friends of the freedom and independence of America, as we are, to raise cash to support the war: because the Whigs ought to be *free* and the *Tories* should be sold." They offer, if set free, to get security to indemnify the State

---

[1] Great Prince, Little Prince, Luke, Caesar, Prue and her three children. Livermore, "Historical Research," p. 116.

in case of their coming to want ; but, though the Lower House was favorable, the Upper one refused to grant the petition.

OPINIONS OF THE FOREFATHERS ON SLAVERY.

One of the earliest in Connecticut to come out boldly against slavery was Rev. Levi Hart of Preston, who, on Sept. 20, 1774, at Farmington, preached a sermon at the meeting of "the Corporation of Freemen," in which he condemned the slave trade and severely criticized slaveholding.[1]

Dr. William Gordon of Roxbury, Mass., though living out of Connecticut, became interested in the abolition of slavery there and sent a plan for its gradual extermination to the "Independent Chronicle" of Nov. 14, 1776, which is very severe on slaveholders and paints the deathbed of one of them.[2]

In the Constitutional Convention[3] of 1787 we have full expression of the views of Roger Sherman and Oliver Ellsworth, two of Connecticut's three delegates. The former said "that the abolition of slavery seemed to be going on in the United States and that the good sense of the several States would probably by degrees complete it."[4] He regarded the slave trade as iniquitous; but, the point of representation having been settled after much difficulty and deliberation,[5] he did not think himself bound to make opposition." He objected, however, to the tax on imported slaves, as implying that slaves were property, and that the tax imposed was too small to prevent importation.[6] He thought that, "as the States were now possessed of the right to import slaves, as the public good did not require it to be taken

---
[1] Trumbull's "Memorial History of Hartford Co.," II., p. 192.
[2] Moore, "Notes on Slavery in Mass.," p. 177.
[3] Connecticut voted for Jefferson's ordinance of 1784.
[4] Livermore, "Historic Research." p. 51.
[5] Madison Papers, V., 391 (Elliot).
[6] Wilson, "Rise and Fall." p. 51.

from them, and as it was expedient to have as few objections as possible to the proposed scheme of government, it would be best to leave the matter as we find it."¹ He said, when Baldwin of Georgia, a man of Connecticut birth, stated his State would not confederate unless allowed to import, that it was better to let the Southern States import slaves² than to lose those States, if they made that a *sine qua non*. He thought it would be the duty of the General Government² to exercise the power of prohibiting importation, if it were given it. He preferred not to use the word slaves in the Constitution, and saw no² more propriety in the public seizing and surrendering a slave than a horse. Ellsworth said, "Let every State import what it pleases. The morality or wisdom of slavery are considerations belonging to the States. What enriches a part enriches the whole, and the States are the best judges of their particular interests. The old Confederation had not meddled with this point, and he did not see any greater necessity for bringing it into the policy of the new one." He had⁴ "never owned a slave and could not judge of the effects of slavery on character." He said, however, that, if it was "to be considered in a moral light, we ought to go further and free those already in the country. As slaves also multiply so fast in Virginia and Maryland, it is cheaper to raise than import them, whilst in the sickly rice swamps, foreign supplies are necessary. If we go no further than is urged, we shall be unjust towards South Carolina and Georgia. Let us not intermeddle. As population increases, poor laborers will be so plenty as to render slaves useless. Provision is already made in Connecticut for abolishing it, and the abolition has already taken place in Massachusetts. As to the dangers of insurrections from foreign influence, that will become a motive to kind treatment of the slaves."⁵

---
¹ Livermore, p. 56.   ² Livermore, p. 60.
³ Elliot, V., pp. 457-461 and 471. Connecticut voted to extend the open period from 1800 to 1808.
⁴ Livermore, p. 57.
⁵ In 1787, Connecticut voted in the Constitutional Convention for the three-fifths compromise.

Mistaken in many respects as these men were, they undoubtedly represented the current opinion of their time.

We find a contrary opinion in the resolves of the Danbury Town Meeting on December 12, 1774, that, " It is with singular pleasure, we notice the second article of the Association, in which it is agreed to import no more Negro slaves, as we cannot but think it a palpable absurdity, so loudly to complain of attempts to enslave us, while we are actually enslaving others, and that we have great reason to apprehend the enslaving the *Africans* is one of the crying sins of our land, for which Heaven is now chastising us. We notice also with pleasure the late Act of our General Assembly, imposing a fine of £100 on any one, who shall import a Negro Slave into this Colony. We could also wish that something further might be done for the relief of such, as are now in a state of slavery in the Colony,[1] and such as may hereafter be born of parents in that unhappy condition."

STATE LEGISLATION ON SLAVERY.

The growth of free ideas went on apace, after the State became independent. In 1780, a bill for gradual emancipation passed the Upper House, was continued until the next session and then, apparently, set aside. It provided that no Indian or colored child, then living and under seven years of age, nor any born afterwards, should be held as a slave beyond the age of twenty-eight.[2] In 1784, however, the measure was passed and emancipation was begun. The Legislature enacted that, "Whereas sound public policy requires that the abolition of slavery should be effected, as soon as may be consistent with the rights of individuals and the public safety and welfare," no negro or mulatto, born after March 1, 1784, should be held as a slave after reaching the age of twenty-five.[3] This regard for the exist-

---

[1] Am. Arch., IV., I., pp. 1038.
[2] Jameson, " Essays in Const. Hist.," p. 296 (Brackett, " Status of the Slave, 1775-1789 ").
[3] Revision of 1808, Title CL., Ch. I., Sec. 13. Fowler, "Hist. Status," p. 85. shows that this really made slaves in the same con-

ing rights of property was shown by the gradual abolition of slavery in Connecticut,[1] the holding of slaves not being absolutely forbidden until 1848, when any one to be a slave must have been sixty-four years old.

In October, 1788, a bill was passed, forbidding any inhabitant of Connecticut to receive on his vessel "any inhabitants of Africa as slaves," under penalty of $1,667 for the use of the vessel and $167 additional for each slave carried.[2] Half of this fine was to go to the plaintiff and half to the State; but, by the act of October, 1798,[3] prosecutions must begin in three years. Furthermore, insurance on ships used in the slave trade, or on slaves carried, is to be void. We have seen the importation of slaves forbidden in this act: the exportation "of any free negro, Indian, or mulatto, or person entitled to freedom at twenty-five," inhabitants of Connecticut, was to be punished by a fine of $334 levied on any who should, as principal or accessory, " kidnap, decoy, or forcibly carry away " such persons from the State. "Any friend of the inhabitant " carried off may prosecute and receive " fit damages," and must give bond to use such rightly for "the injured inhabitant,"[4] or family. This prohibition was not to prevent persons removing from the State from taking their slaves with them, nor to prevent persons living in Connecticut from sending their slaves out of the State, on ordinary and necessary business. This sale of slaves out of the State was soon stopped, for, in May, 1792, the law was so changed that the taking a slave from the State, or assistance therein, was punishable with a

---

dition as apprentices. and claims the law was passed partly through economical reasons. as there were more laborers than employment.

[1] In October, 1788, owners must file certificate of birth of each slave within six months thereof, or pay $7 for each month's delay, half to complainant and half to poor of town. October, 1789, the latter half was to go to the State. Revision of 1808, Title CL., Ch. V., Sec. 5, and Ch. VI.

[2] Revision of 1808, Title CL., Ch. V., Sec. 1. Penalty changed to $170 and $1700 by Revision of 1821, Title 93, Sec. 7. Penalty was originally £1000. Root's Reports, I., xxxi.

[3] Revision of 1808, Title CI., Ch. III.

[4] Revision of 1808, Title CL., Ch. V., Secs. 3-4. Penalty changed to $350 in Revision of 1821, Sec. 6.

like fine of $334, half of which should go to the plaintiff and half to the State. Notes, bonds, or mortgages given in payment for slaves thus sold out of the State were to be void. The same exemptions as to persons removing from the State or sending their slaves out temporarily, were made as in the former law.[1]

At the same session of the Assembly, the age of the slave at manumission was limited to the period between twenty-five and forty-five years, and the certificate given at emancipation by the selectmen was ordered to be recorded in the Town Records.[2] This somewhat reactionary act, modifying the law of 1702, designed to regulate the giving of freedom, was followed in five years by one still further limiting the bounds of slavery; for in May, 1797, it was enacted that no negro or mulatto born after August, 1797, should be a slave, after reaching the age of twenty-one.[3]

Here the laws with regard to slavery remained without essential change for many years. Not until 1833 do we find another important act passed in regard to slavery, and then, under the influence of the outcry against Miss Prudence Crandall, the Legislature put on the statute-book the most shameful law we meet in our study.[4] It stated that, "whereas attempts have been made to establish literary institutions in this State, for the instruction of colored persons belonging to other States and countries, which would tend to the great increase of the colored population of the State and thereby to the injury of the people," any person establishing such a school without the consent in writing of the selectmen and civil authority of the town, should pay a fine of $100 to the State Treasurer for the first offense and double for each

---

[1] Revision of 1808, Title CL., Ch. VI., Secs. 1, 2, 3.
[2] Revision of 1808, Title CL., Ch. II. Free negroes could vote until the Constitution of 1818 restricted the suffrage to white males.
[3] Revision of 1808. Title CL., Ch. III.
[4] May 24, 1833. Act of 1833, Ch.   Sec. 1. Sec. 2 provided that a colored person not an inhabitant of Connecticut, residing in a town for education, might be removed as any other alien. Sec. 3 provided that the evidence of such colored person is both admissible and compulsory against the teacher.

succeeding one, the fines increasing in geometrical progression. The law was not destined to be a blot upon any of the States' codes, but was repealed in 1838 by the Legislature, under the leadership of Francis Gillette,[1] a young representative from Hartford, who was afterwards United States Senator. That same Legislature passed resolutions against the annexation of Texas, the slave trade in the District of Columbia, and in favor of the right of petition. Nay more, that same year was passed the "Act for the Fulfilment of the Obligations of this State imposed by the Constitution of the United States in regard to persons held to service or labor in one State and escaping into another, and to secure the right of trial by jury in the cases herein mentioned."[2] Prof. W. C. Fowler called this law a "nullification"[3] of the United States Act of 1793, which provided that the owner or his attorney could take the fugitive slave before any magistrate of the county, city, or town wherein the arrest might be made, and, on proof by oral testimony or affidavit, taken before and certified to by a magistrate of any State or Territory, the magistrate must give a certificate, which should be sufficient warrant for removing the slave from the State.

Let us see now how Connecticut fulfilled her obligations, in this early personal liberty law. Instead of following the provisions of the United States law, she enacted that the captured fugitive should be brought before the county or city court on a writ of *habeas corpus*, and no magistrate not having the power to issue that writ should give the claimant any warrant or certificate, under penalty of $500. When he arrived at court, the claimant must pay all fees in advance and must, "by affidavit, set forth minutely" the ground of

---

[1] Wilson, "Rise and Fall of the Slave Power," I., 372. The Legislature, however, by a vote of 105 to 33, rejected a constitutional amendment allowing negroes the suffrage. Niles' Reg., Vol. 54, p. 193. In 1842 the State again protested against the annexation of Texas. Niles' Reg., Vol. 62, p. 140.
[2] Revision of 1838, Title 97, Ch. II.
[3] Local Law in Mass. and Conn., p. 98.

his claim to the slave's services, the time of the slave's escape, and the place where the slave then was, or was believed to be. The judge was next to allow necessary time for further proof and, meantime, commit the fugitive to the custody of the sheriff. The questions of fact were to be tried by a jury, on which no one was to sit "who believes there is not, constitutionally or legally, a slave in the land," in this showing the early distrust of the Abolitionists. If the claimant does not prove the claim, he is liable to the payment of costs and damages; if he does prove it, he may take the slave from the State, but must, "without unnecessary delay," take him by the "direct route" to his home. In the same act, the law against transporting slaves from the State, save as above, is made universal and the penalty for its violation fixed at $500, to go to any one prosecuting. Any fugitive arrested, contrary to the act, may have a writ of *habeas corpus* sued out by his next friend; and, as an afterthought, at the very end, we read that nothing in this act shall extend to the United States Courts.

As the feeling grew more bitter, even this law was felt to be too much of a yielding in principle and, in 1844,[1] the Legislature decided that no Judge, Justice of the Peace, or other officer should issue a warrant "for the arrest or detention of any person escaping into this State, claimed to be fugitive from labor or service as a slave," or grant a certificate to the claimant. Such papers, if issued, are to be void, but, as before, the people soothed their consciences with the belief they were fulfilling their obligations, by saying "nothing herein shall interfere with United States officers."[2]

In 1847,[3] by a great majority, the State rejected a proposal

---

[1] Compilation of 1854, Title 51, Sec. 5. The preamble stated that "it has been decided by the Supreme Court of the United States since" 1838 "that both the duty and the power of legislation on that subject pertains exclusively to the National government."

[2] In 1845 the Legislature of Connecticut protested against the admission of Texas as a Slave State. Niles' Reg., Vol. 69, p. 246.

[3] The vote was, for. 5,353; against, 19,148. Over half the legal voters did not vote. Niles' Reg., Vol. 73, Nov. 6, 1847. Fowler, p. 152.

to allow colored men the ballot, but the next year[1] it decreed, what was already almost accomplished by the action of former laws, "that no person shall hereafter be held in slavery in this State," that emancipated slaves must be supported by their masters,[2] and that no slave shall be brought into Connecticut. Thus Connecticut became in law a Free State, as she long had been in fact. When the fugitive slave law of 1850 was passed, the rising tide of indignation swept over Connecticut. Here and there some resisted the torrent and organized Union Saving Meetings, like the one the famous Rev. N. W. Taylor addressed at New Haven, deprecating agitation, counseling obedience, declaring that he had not been able to discover that the article in the Constitution for the rendition of fugitives was " contrary to the law of nature, to the law of nations, or the law of God," and claiming that it was "lawful to deliver up fugitives for the high, the great, the momentous interests of the Southern States."[3] But the majority sympathized rather with Gov. H. B. Harrison, when he introduced his "personal liberty bill" in the Senate of 1854, and "avowed his belief that it would render the fugitive slave law inoperative in Connecticut." The Hon. Henry C. Deming, in opposing the bill, said, though it was "nicely drawn," he thought it conflicted in spirit with the United States Constitution, as it undoubtedly did, and that "it was not in equity and justice deserved by our Southern brethren, if they behave pretty well." The advocates of the bill used no such mild terms. The Hon. John Boyd, late Secretary of State, said "desperate diseases require desperate remedies." He had "some faith in the homoeopathic remedy that like requires like," and, as he believed "the exigencies of the time" demanded it, he thanked Mr. Harrison for introducing the bill. He added, "if Shy-

---

[1] Compilation of 1854, Title 51, Secs. 1 and 2. *Vide* Conn. Repts., II., 355.
[2] Remember all such must have been over sixty-four years of age.
[3] Wilson, "Rise and Fall of the Slave Power," II., 318.
[4] Fowler, "Local Law in Mass. and Conn.," pp. 98-99. It was introduced about June 25.

lock claims his pound of flesh, he must be careful not to take any of the blood." Judge Sanford saw in the bill "new and important principles, which he believed were entirely constitutional and would be so decided by the Supreme Court." Ex-Gov. Wm. S. Miner could not find a "single line, sentence, or word" unconstitutional in the bill. Judge Sanford spoke again and again, using such language as this: that he thought the South had driven this matter so fast that it had "driven us back to our reserved rights, if we had any." He would occupy the last inch the Constitution left them, come square up to the line, but not one step over. He would oppose the fugitive slave law by any means in his power within the limits of the Constitution. He said, with great clearness, dignity, and force, that the bill was constitutional, that the emergencies of the times demanded such a law; he portrayed the odious features of the fugitive slave law and said the slave-catcher was the most despicable of men. At the same time a bill was introduced, which, however, did not pass, prohibiting the use of any court-house, jail, or other public building for the trial or confinement of fugitive slaves. To this, Mr. Boyd proposed an amendment that a building used for such a purpose should "be rased to the foundation and remain a perpetual ruin." Even the excited Senate had good sense enough to vote this frantic proposition down.

The law as passed, entitled "An Act for the Defense of Liberty in this State," provided that "any person, who shall falsely and maliciously pretend that any free person is a slave, intending to remove him from Connecticut, shall pay a fine of $5000 and be imprisoned five years in the State Prison." In trials, two credible persons, or equivalent evidence, were required to prove the defendant a slave, and depositions were not to be received as evidence. Witnesses falsely representing free persons as slaves are to receive the punishment mentioned above, and, with the intention to satisfy their consciences that they were not violating United States law, the legislators added that any person hindering an officer from the arrest of a fugitive, or aiding an accused person to escape, was to be imprisoned one year in State's prison. The last section of the bill contained an interesting reminder of colonial customs, in providing that the act should not cover the case of apprentices.

Though slavery is still found as a title in the Revision[1] of 1866, the last act on the subject was passed in 1857, and with that the statutory history of slavery in Connecticut may well be ended. At that time it was enacted that "any person held to service as a slave in any other State or country," and not being a fugitive from another of the United States, "coming into this State, or being therein, shall forthwith become and be free."

CASES ADJUDICATED IN THE HIGHER COURTS WITH REFERENCE TO SLAVERY.

The question as to the manumission of slaves by service in the Continental Army with the master's consent, was decided in the case of *Jack Arabas* versus *Ivers*.[2] Ivers, the master, permitted Arabas to enlist in the army. He served through the war and was discharged at its end, when Ivers again claimed him. He fled to the eastward, was overtaken and brought back to New Haven, where he was put in the jail for safekeeping. He sued out a "habeas corpus" and the court granted it, "upon the ground that he was a free man, absolutely manumitted from his master by enlisting and serving in the army." It was a fine idea, that he who helped to free his country could not be a slave.

The only other case in the Connecticut reports as to manumission is *Geer* versus *Huntington*,[3] where the plaintiff claimed a negro as his slave by a bill of sale from his former mistress, while the defendant claimed that the mistress had told him he should be servant to no one but her and should be free at the age of twenty-five. As he had passed that

---

[1] Title LVIII., Secs. 1-6. [2] Root's Reports, I., p. 92, 1784.
[3] Root's Reports, II., 364.

age before he left her service, the court held him to have been freed, by a liberal interpretation of her promise.

The only case I have found tried in Connecticut in regard to the Slave Trade, save the famous Amistad case, to be treated later, is that of the *United States* versus *John Smith*.[1] It was an action to recover double the value of Smith's interest in over one hundred negro slaves, transported in the brig Heroine, of which he was sole owner and master, from Africa to Havana, and there sold, contrary to the Act of Congress of May 10, 1800. The Heroine was in Africa between Dec. 1, 1805 and April 1, 1806, and, arriving at Havana before June 1, Smith sold the slaves before the end of that month for not less than $10,000, so action was brought for $20,000. One of the crew was offered as a witness by the government; but Smith's attorney objected to this testimony on the ground that it would incriminate the man and subject him to a fine of not over $2000 and two years imprisonment, according to the above-mentioned Act of Congress. The government said they had entered a *nolle prosequi* in his case and it was too late to institute another proceeding against him. The defense pleaded that the witness had fled from justice and that in such case the statute of limitations would not hold. Further, he might be excused from testifying, as he was unwilling; but the judge ruled that a witness could not plead his wrong-doing as a defense and must testify. However, there was a verdict for the defendant, as the judge charged the jury that the offense was completed when the vessel arrived at Havana, not when the slaves were sold, and the prosecution, though begun within the prescribed period, two years, of the latter date, was not within two years of the former.

The most frequent cause of negroes appearing in cases before the Supreme Court was the law of settlement. When negroes became infirm and were penniless, it was an important question who should support them, and from this several

---

[1] Day's Reports, IV., p. 121. U. S. Circuit Court, Hartford, Sept., 1809. Fowler's "Hist. Status," pp. 16-18, has interesting facts on slave trade in Conn.

cases arose. The first of these,[1] *Wilson et al.* vs. *Hinkley et al.*, in the Tolland County Court, was a case of an appeal from a judgment of a Justice of the Peace. In this court, Hinkley and others, selectmen of the town of Tolland, sued the selectmen of the town of Coventry for support of Amy Caesar and her children. This Amy, daughter of an Indian woman, was born in Tolland, and lived with a citizen of that town as servant till eighteen years of age. Then she was set at liberty and, after four years more in Tolland, married Timothy Caesar, also a child of an Indian woman and slave to a citizen of Mansfield, where they lived nine months. Thence they removed to Coventry, Timothy being granted permission to do so by his master. There they lived eighteen months, since which time Amy and her children had apparently lived in Tolland. Tolland's claim for reimbursement was resisted by Coventry, which said the former masters of Amy and Timothy should support them. The court decided that Timothy, "being born of a free woman, a native of the land, was not a slave," applying apparently the old civil law maxim. "Nor" was he "a servant bound for time, nor an apprentice under age, nor under disability to gain settlement by commorancy"; therefore, by residence in Coventry over a year he had gained settlement for himself and wife, and, as she was never a "slave or servant bought for time," Coventry must pay the expense of her support.

The next case was also one in which the same town of Tolland was interested; *Ebenezer Kingsbury* vs. *Tolland*.[2] Joseph Kingsbury, of Norwich, bought two native Africans, Cuff and Phyllis, as "servants for life," and gave them to his wife. She died, December, 1773, freeing them. In 1775, with the consent of Ebenezer Kingsbury, their former mistress's sole executor, they removed to Tolland and, after living there nine years, came to want and were supported by the town. The town brought suit against Kingsbury and won in the County Court; but in the Court of Appeals lost its case, on the technicality that he was sued personally and not

---

[1] Kirby Reports, 202. [2] Root's Reports, February, 1796.

as executor. The court, however, in an *obiter dictum*, intimated the personal representatives and next of kin were liable, if sued as such, for the support of freed slaves, if there were sufficient assets.

A third case was *Bolton* vs. *Haddam*,[1] by which was determined that a slave was domiciled with his master and, if manumitted in any way, continued an inhabitant of the same town as before, unless he became legally settled elsewhere.

Twenty years now pass before we find another such case; then, November, 1817, was decided the case of *Windsor* vs. *Hartford*.[2] This rather important case regarded the residence of a negress, Fanny Libbet, and her two illegitimate children. Fanny, herself illegitimate, was born in Hartford in 1785 and, at the age of three, was given by her master to his son in Wethersfield. There she lived until twenty-five years of age, when her term of service by law expired. Her mother had been sold to a citizen of Windsor in 1795 and was emancipated by him in 1801. Fanny went to her mother as soon as she could, and there her two children were born. Windsor supported them for a while and then sued Hartford, on the ground that Fanny, born after March 1, 1784, was never a slave and so took her settlement from her birthplace, Hartford. The court so decided, stating that "she is to be considered as a free person and never was a slave," an important interpretation of the act of 1784. Her residence in Wethersfield was that of an apprentice, and she had never gained settlement in Windsor. As she never had been a slave, her former master was not liable to her support.

Soon after was tried the case of the *Town of Columbia* vs. *Williams et alium*. A citizen of Groton had left a slave, Adam, who had, after his master's decease, removed to Columbia and there became a town charge. The town sued the heirs of Williams, and they claimed that the suit was improperly brought, that Groton ought have been sued, as Adam had a settlement with his master there, which town

---

[1] Root's Reports, II., p. 517. February, 1797. Tolland County.
[2] Conn. Reports, II., p. 355.
[3] Conn. Reports, III., 467, October 28, 1820.

could then have recovered from them. As it was admitted that Adam had never been manumitted, the court sustained the claims of the defendants, and the town, on this point, lost its case and a new trial was ordered, which seems never to have come off.

Flora,[1] slave of Elisha Pitkin, gave rise to two cases. *Pitkin et al.* vs. *Pitkin et al.*, the first, was brought by the executors of Elisha Pitkin against certain of his heirs. He executed a deed of gift of all his real estate to the plaintiffs and defendants in 1816, but kept it in his possession until his death, three years later. When he died, he bequeathed his remaining property by testament to the plaintiffs and certain of the defendants, to be equally divided among them, they being enjoined to take care of Flora and bear the expense equally, or to have the executors reserve sufficient estate for her support. The executors claimed they paid " large sums " for her support, supposing there was sufficient estate; but, at final settlement, found not enough was left outside of the real estate conveyed by deed. This they ask the court to order sold, sufficiently to provide for Flora's support. The defendants demurred, and their demurrer being sustained, the plaintiffs carry the case to the higher court. The plaintiffs contended that, "where there is service for life there must be support for life," and, therefore, the support of the slave was a charge upon the estate, that Mr. Pitkin's intention was to have her supported, that it was the duty of the executors to support her, and they were consequently not volunteers and had a superior equity to that of the defendants, and that the court should decide the case according to its equities. The defendants said Mr. Pitkin did not charge Flora's support on the real estate, that the executors were volunteers, having nothing to do with the real estate, and that, if the land should be liable, it should be so decided in a probate, not in a chancery court. The court decided in favor of the defendants,

---

[1] Conn. Reports, VII., p. 315, June, 1829, and VIII., 392, June, 1831.

[2] Probably not all, though of this I am not absolutely sure.

on this last contention, and on the ground that it could not foresee what sums might be needed for her support, and hence could not determine on the quantity of land to be sold.

Having lost their case, the executors seem to have given up trying to support Flora and to have endeavored to throw the expense on the town of East Hartford, which sued them in 1831, alleging that it had supported Flora three years. The defendants demurred that the selectmen were not obliged to support her, and as volunteers they cannot recover, for " the duty of support rests on the master alone," and he is only liable to the town for the support of emancipated slaves. " Slavery is not founded in reason and justice, like the relations of husband and wife." Thirdly, as the supplies were not furnished in Elisha Pitkin's lifetime, the defendants should be sued as owners, not executors. The prosecution, on the other hand, asserted that the relation of master and slave is recognized by statute law; during the continuance of this relation the master is liable for support of slave, which slave if unemancipated remains part of the estate; that a needy slave must be relieved by the town in which is his settlement, for which relief recovery is to be had at law. Judge Daggett, in his majority opinion, confined himself to the obligation of the selectmen for her support. He said the only cases where the town would have to support a slave were when both master and slave were paupers, or a slave emancipated in accordance with the act of 1792 should become such. In this suit neither was the fact, and the town was a volunteer and could no more recover than if it had supported a wife or child of a man of means. Chief Justice Hosmer agreed with this reasoning, from which Judge Peters dissented, though he agreed with the decision. He said, " The relation of master and servant, or qualified slavery, has existed in Connecticut from time immemorial and has been tolerated (not sanctioned) by the legislature. But absolute slavery, where the master has unlimited power over the life of the slave, has never been permitted in this State." He continued, Flora at Mr. Pitkin's death, not being specially devised, vested as a chattel in the executors. "They alone could sell her; they became her masters and she their slave, and they alone were to maintain her." He thought, however, she ought to be maintained by the town as a vagrant, when the town could recover by implied promise; basing his decision for the defendants, on the technicality that, "when an executor covenants or promises, he binds himself personally and not the heirs or estate of the testator, therefore they should not have been sued as executors, but as persons."

Judge Williams filed a dissenting opinion, in which Judge Bissell concurred. He placed the chief importance on the implied promise, stating, "that slavery has existed in this State cannot be denied, and a few solitary cases still exist, to attest to the melancholy truth...The man who had a right to all the time and services and even offspring of his unhappy slave, must, of course, be bound to maintain him." Executors are liable for debts arising after death of the testator, "where the demand arises from an obligation existing upon the testator in his life." Such an obligation was the support of this slave, which, as personal property, vested in the executors. He thought that it was not necessary to sue them personally, that the *onus probandi* rested on them, that there were no assets. The town was not a volunteer, for "the woman must be relieved by the town where she was, or starve." He quoted a statute providing that "all poor and impotent persons," without estate or relatives, "shall be provided for and supported by the town." The town cannot wait to hunt up the persons legally liable, before rendering aid. "The owner of the slave is primarily liable, and it is only his neglect of duty which makes the defendants liable at all, and it is admitted that, in consequence of that neglect, the defendants would be responsible to any *individual* who supplied the necessities of the slave," and the judge then said he saw no reason why the town also should not recover. His opinion, leaving the interpretation of the statutes and basing itself on abstract considerations, stated that, "by the principles of natural justice they are bound to refund, and I am not satisfied that any technical rule of law can be interposed to prevent it."

The opinions in this case seemed important enough to devote some space to it. The next case[1] we note is that of *Colchester* vs. *Lyme*, for support of Jenny. She had belonged to a citizen of Lyme until fifty-six years of age, when she was emancipated and went to live in Colchester. Coming to want, the town sued her old residence for her support, claiming that, as she was over forty-five when emancipated, the liability of her master to support her continued, and, " while the liability of the master to support the slave remains, the incapacity of the slave to acquire a new settlement remains also." This the defense denied, and the court decided in their favor. The opinion stated: " If she had been white, or never a slave, she would have had a settlement in Colchester. Does the fact she was once a slave alter matters? There was nothing in the statute (of 1777) which in the least impaired the right of the master to give entire freedom to his slave at any time." The want of a certificate only continued the master's liability to support the slave. " By relinquishing all claims to service and obedience," he " effectually emancipated her, and thus she became *sui juris* and entitled to all the rights and privileges of other free citizens of the State, among which the right of acquiring a new place of settlement was the most important....The town where the emancipated slave belongs or has a settlement, is the town empowered by statute to recover from the master or his heirs,...and if Colchester is such a town, then Colchester only can recover from the former master or his representatives."[2]

The last case of the kind is *New Haven* vs. *Huntington*, decided as late as 1852, in which it was adjudged that the settlement of a free woman in Connecticut is not superseded by marriage with a slave of another State, nor by his subsequent emancipation, unless the laws of the other State (which

---

[1] Conn. Reports, XIII., p. 274, July, 1839.
[2] *Guilford* vs. *Oxford*, Conn. Reports, IX., 321, is a suit for the support of an illegitimate free mulatto.

in this case was New York) so provide, and her settlement is communicated both to legitimate and illegitimate children born in Connecticut after the marriage.[1]

Considerable attention has been given to these cases, as they illustrate important principles of the laws of the State and show how the judges interpreted those laws.

MISS PRUDENCE CRANDALL AND HER SCHOOL.

In the autumn of 1831,[2] Miss Crandall, a Quakeress, residing in the southern part of Canterbury, opened a girls' school in that town. She had taught at Plainfield successfully, and moved to Canterbury, at the request of some prominent citizens, buying a house on the Green. Her school was a success from the outset, until she received as pupil a colored girl, Sarah Harris, about seventeen years of age, the daughter of a respectable man who owned a small farm near the centre. The girl was a member of the village church, and had been at the district school, in the same class as some of Miss Crandall's pupils. She now wished "to get a little more learning—enough to teach colored children." Previous to this admission to the school, Miss Crandall had employed as a servant a "nice colored girl," Marcia, who was afterward married to Charles Harris, the brother of Sarah. Young Harris took Garrison's "Liberator" and loaned it to Marcia, who used frequently to show the paper to Miss Crandall. "Having been taught from early childhood the sin of slavery," as she wrote in 1869, "my sympathies were greatly aroused," and so Miss Crandall agreed to receive Sarah Harris as a day scholar. "By this act," she continued, in the same letter, "I gave great offense. The wife of an Episcopalian clergyman, who lived in the village, told me that, if I continued that colored girl in my school, it

---

[1] Conn. Reports, XXII.
[2] The chief authorities are Larned's "Hist. Windham Co.," Vol. II., Book IX., Chap. III., pp. 491 sq.; S. J. May, "Recollections of the Anti-slavery Conflict," pp. 47-71, which Wilson, "Rise and Fall," I., pp. 240-245, and Williams, "Hist. Negro Race," II., pp. 149-156, almost entirely followed; Crandall vs. Conn., Conn. Reports.

could not be sustained. I replied to her '*that it might sink, then, for I should not turn her out.*' I very soon found that some of my school would not return, if the colored girl was retained. Under the circumstances, I made up my mind that, if it were possible, I would teach colored girls exclusively." Now, though Miss Crandall was undoubtedly shamefully treated by the people of the town, they nevertheless had just ground of complaint from the course she pursued. Because some of her patrons were offended at the entrance of one colored girl into her school, she determined to give up teaching white girls entirely, and to bring a number of colored children into the most aristocratic part of the town, while the people who had received her most kindly and had consented to act as visitors to her school were not regarded. She consulted leading Abolitionists in New York and Boston, but no one in the town, whose interests were most immediately concerned in the opening of such a school. Some irritation might therefore have been expected, but the conduct of the townspeople went beyond all bounds and was thoroughly disgraceful. Miss Crandall's conduct, on the other hand, apart from her initial lack of consideration for the judgment of those around her, was consistent, courageous, and praiseworthy.

When she announced her purpose to open a school for "young ladies and little misses of color," dismay seized all. A committee of four of the chief men of the village visited her to remonstrate with her, and, on her proving obdurate, a town meeting was called for March 9, 1833, to meet in the Congregational Meeting-house. Miss Crandall had not shown a conciliating spirit. When Esquire Frost had labored to convince her of the impropriety of her step "in a most kind and affecting manner," and "hinted at danger from these leveling opinions" and from intermarriage of whites and blacks, Miss Crandall at once replied, "Moses had a black wife." She asked Rev. Samuel J. May, pastor of the Unitarian Church in Brooklyn, George W. Benson, the President, and Arnold Buffum, Agent of the New England

Anti-Slavery Society, to present her cause at the town meeting. Judge Rufus Adams offered the following resolutions: "Whereas, it hath been publicly announced that a school is to be opened in this town on the first Monday of April next, using the language of the advertisement, 'for young ladies and little misses of color,' or in other words for the people of color, the obvious tendency of which would be to collect, within the town of Canterbury, large numbers of persons from other States, whose characters and habits might be various and unknown to us, thereby rendering insecure the persons, property, and reputations of our citizens. Under such circumstances, our silence might be construed into an approbation of the project. Thereupon:

"Resolved, that the locality of a school for the people of color, at any place within the limits of this town, for the admission of persons of foreign jurisdiction, meets with our unqualified disapprobation, and it is to be understood that the inhabitants of Canterbury protest against it in the most earnest manner.

"Resolved, that a committee be now appointed, to be composed of the civil authority and selectmen, who shall make known to the person contemplating the establishment of said school, the sentiments and objections entertained by this meeting, in reference to said school, pointing out to her the injurious effects and incalculable evils resulting from such an establishment within this town, and persuade her to abandon the project."

The Hon. Andrew T. Judson, a Democratic politician, later Congressman and United States District Judge, who resided next to Miss Crandall, and who had been horrified at the prospect of having a school of negro girls as his neighbor, addressed the meeting "in a tone of bitter and relentless hostility" to Miss Crandall. After him, Rev. Mr. May and Mr. Buffum presented a letter from Miss Crandall to the Moderator, asking that they might be heard in her behalf. Judson and others at once interposed and prevented their speaking. They had intended to propose that, if the town would repay Miss Crandall the cost of her house and give her time to remove, she would open her school in some more retired part of the town or vicinity. Doubtless this would not have been satisfactory to the people, but that does not excuse the lack of courtesy on the part of the people in refusing to hear what Miss Crandall's agents had to propose. The resolutions were passed, but nothing deterred the fearless woman. She opened her school with from ten to twenty girls as pupils.[1] This still more enraged the townspeople, and, at a second town meeting, it was resolved: " That the *establishment or rendezvous*, falsely denominated a school, was designed by its projectors, as the *theatre*, as the place to promulgate their disgusting doctrines of amalgamation and their pernicious sentiments of subverting the Union. Their pupils were to have been congregated here from *all quarters*, under the false pretense of *educating them;* but really to SCATTER FIREBRANDS, *arrows, and death* among brethren of our own blood." A committee of ten was appointed to draw up and circulate a petition to the General Assembly, " deprecating the evil consequences of bringing from other States and other towns, people of color for any purpose, and more especially for the purpose of disseminating the principles and doctrines opposed to the benevolent colonizing system." Other towns were asked to prefer " petitions for the same laudable object." The people had completely lost their heads and were mad with rage and fear. As a result of this petition, the shameful act of May 24, 1833, before referred to, was passed.

The conduct of the people of Canterbury was even more indefensible than their words. They hunted up an obsolete vagrant law, providing that the selectmen might warn any non-inhabitant of the State to depart, demanding $1.67 for each week they should thereafter stay, and, if the fine were not paid, or the person were still in the town after ten days, he should be whipped on the bare body, with not over ten

---

[1] Pupils came from Philadelphia, New York, Providence, and Boston, says May.

stripes. An endeavor was made to put this law in force against Miss Crandall's pupils, and one of them, Ann Eliza Hammond, a girl of seventeen, from Providence, was arrested. Rev. Mr. May and other residents of Brooklyn gave bonds for $10,000, so the attempt was given up.

The lawless treatment of the school and scholars was worse than the legal one. The stage-driver refused to carry the pupils to the school, the neighbors refused to give Miss Crandall a pail of water, though they knew their sons had filled her well with stable refuse the night before. Boys followed the school with horns and hootings on the streets, and stones and rotten eggs were thrown at Miss Crandall's windows. A systematic policy of boycotting and intimidation was carried out. The village stores were closed against the school. Men went to Miss Crandall's father, a mild and peaceable Quaker living in the southern part of the town, and told him, " when lawyers, courts and jurors are leagued against you, it will be easy to raise a mob and tear down your house." He was terrified and wished his daughter to yield, but she boldly refused. He petitioned the Legislature against the passage of the act of May 24, 1833, but in vain. The sentiment of men from other towns was that they would not want a negro school on their common.

After the passage of the act, two leading citizens told him " your daughter will be taken up the same way as for stealing a horse or for burglary. Her property will not be taken, but she will be put in jail, not having the liberty of the yard. There is no mercy to be shown about it."

A few days later, Messrs. May and George W. Benson visited Miss Crandall, to advise with her as to the fine and imprisonment provided by the act as penalty for teaching colored children not residing in the State. As Wilson puts it, the result of their conference was a determination to leave her in the hands " of those with whom the hideous act originated."

On June 27, 1833, Miss Crandall was arrested, brought before a Justice of the Peace and committed for trial before the County Court in August. Mr. May and her friends were told that she was in the sheriff's hands and would be put in jail unless bonds were given. They resolved not to do so, but to force the framers of the statute to give bonds themselves or commit her to jail. The sheriff and jailer saw this would be a disgrace and lingered; but her friends were firm, and Miss Crandall spent the night in a cell which had last been occupied by a condemned murderer. The next morning bonds were given, by whom it does not appear; but the fact of her incarceration caused a revulsion of popular feeling in her favor. Mr. Arthur Tappan wrote at once to Mr. May, indorsing his conduct, authorizing him to spare no reasonable cost in defense at his expense and to employ the ablest counsel.

The Hon. Wm. W. Ellsworth, Calvin Goddard, and Henry Strong were retained and prepared to argue that the laws were unconstitutional. Mr. Tappan took such interest in the case that he left his business to have a personal interview with Miss Crandall and Mr. May. To the latter he said, " The cause of the whole oppressed race of our country is to be much affected by the decision of this question. You are almost helpless without the press. You must issue a paper, publish it largely, send it to all persons whom you know in the country and State, and to all the principal newspapers of the country. Many will subscribe for it and contribute largely to its support, and I will pay whatever it may cost." Mr. May took the advice and started the "Unionist," with Charles C. Burleigh, of Plainfield, as editor.

On August 23, the case of *The State* versus *Crandall* was tried at Brooklyn, before Judge Joseph Eaton; Messrs. A. T. Judson, Jonathan Welch, Esq., and J. Bulkley appearing as counsel for the State. Mr. Judson denied that negroes were citizens in States where they were not enfranchised, and asked why men should be educated who could not be freemen. The defense claimed that the law conflicted with the clause of the United States Constitution allowing to citizens of one State equal rights in others. The judge charged the jury that the law was constitutional, but the jury disagreed, standing seven for conviction and five for acquittal.

The prosecution did not wait for a new trial in December, but went before the Connecticut Superior Court. Judge Daggett presided over the October Session. According to Mr. May, he was known to be an advocate of the new law, and in the course of an elaborate opinion said, "it would be a perversion of the terms and the well known rule of construction to say that slaves, free-blacks, or Indians were *citizens* within the meaning of the Constitution." The jury gave a verdict against Miss Crandall and her counsel appealed to the Court of Errors. It heard the case on July 22,[1] 1834, and reversed the previous decision, on the ground of "insufficiency of information," and that there was no allegation that the school was set up without a license, and so left the constitutional question unsettled.

Meantime the school had been continued, W. H. Burleigh and his sister and Miss Crandall's sister Almira assisting in the work.[2] They even had at times a sort of exhibition of the pupils' progress. The opposition to the school in Canterbury did not diminish; the trustees of the Congregational church refused to let Miss Crandall and her pupils worship there. The Friends Meeting at Black Hill and the Baptist church at Packerville, both a few miles off, received them, but were almost the only ones to show kindness. Even the physicians of the place refused to attend Miss Crandall's household. After the opponents failed in the courts, they resorted more than before to violent means. Early in September an attempt was made to burn her house, and her enemies went so far as to arrest a colored man she had employed to do some work for her, and to claim she had the fire started to excite sympathy. A still more dastardly attack was made on the building on September 9, by a body of men, who at night broke all the windows and doors with

---

[1] A. T. Judson and C. F. Cleaveland for State, W. W. Ellsworth and Calvin Goddard for Miss Crandall.

[2] Larned, II., p. 499.

clubs and crowbars. The house was left nearly uninhabitable. Miss Crandall's friends all advised her to give up the school, and she did so, sending the twenty girls then composing it to their homes. Mr. May said when he gave the advice to yield, the words blistered his lips and his bosom glowed with indignation. "I felt ashamed of Connecticut," he wrote in his Memoirs, "ashamed of my State, ashamed of my country, ashamed of my color."

Miss Crandall was soon after married to Mr. Calvin Philleo and left Canterbury. The town, feeling obliged to justify its conduct, spread upon its records the following resolve: "That the Government of the United States, the nation with all its institutions, of right belong to the white men, who now possess them,...that our appeal to the Legislature of our own State, in a case of such peculiar mischief, was not only due to ourselves, but to the obligations devolving upon us under the Constitution. To have been silent would have been participating in the wrongs intended.... We rejoice that the appeal was not in vain."

Here ends the wretched story. But its results were far-reaching. As Larned, the historian of Windham County, well writes, if Miss Crandall did not succeed in educating negro girls, she did in altering the opinions of that part of Connecticut, which became the strongest anti-slavery part of the State.

Nancy Jackson vs. Bulloch.

This celebrated case, interpreting the acts of 1774 and 1784 and practically ending slavery in Connecticut, deserves especial notice. In this case, the Supreme Court of the State, by a bare majority, decided that the statutes just mentioned "were designed to terminate slavery in Connecticut and that they are sufficient for that purpose. The act of 1774 aimed a blow at the increase of slaves, that of 1784 struck at the existence of slavery. The former was intended to weaken the system; the latter to destroy it. The former lopped off a limb from the trunk; the latter struck a deadly blow at the root, and ever since it has withered and decayed, and, with the exception of here and there a dying limb, slavery has disappeared from our State and will in a short time be known only in our history, unless indeed it is to revive and flourish, by the construction we shall now give to the statutes. To us it appears as if there was nothing in the intent of the Legislature, or in the words of the act, which requires such a construction."[1]

The facts of the case were as follows: J. S. Bulloch, a citizen of Georgia, owned a slave, Nancy Jackson, born in Georgia in 1813. In June, 1835, he came to Connecticut and settled at Hartford, to live there temporarily while his children were being educated.

Since that time Nancy had been residing with Bulloch's family in Hartford, while he had only spent the summer in Connecticut, returning to Georgia for the winter. Nancy, through her next friend, brought an action for unjust confinement against Bulloch, and, a writ of Habeas Corpus being sued out, the case was heard in June, 1837. Chief Justice Williams, in giving the opinion of the Court, went over the whole law of slavery, and this makes the decision more valuable. He took the broad ground " that every human being has a right to liberty, as well as to life and property, and to enjoy the fruit of his own labor; that slavery is contrary to the principles of natural right and to the great law of love; that it is founded on injustice and fraud and can be supported only by the provisions of positive law, are positions which it is not necessary to prove." The defendant admitted that slavery was local and must be governed by State law, and that neither the fugitive slave clause nor any other clause of the United States Constitution applies to this case; therefore he can have no higher claims than an inhabitant of a foreign State. "It cannot be denied that in this State we have not been entirely free from the evil of slavery....A small remnant still remains to remind us of the fact.... How or when it was introduced into this State we are not

---

[1] Conn. Reports, XII., p. 38.

informed....It probably crept in silently, until it became sanctioned by custom or usage." He went on to state that if it depended entirely on that fact, it might be enquired whether the custom was "reasonable," but for a century slavery has been somewhat recognized by statute and thus has received the implied sanction of the Legislature. He then takes up the claims of the plaintiff's counsel that the slaves are freed by the first article of the Bill of Rights, which states that all men are equal in rights "when they form a social compact." This, says the Judge, does not apply, as slaves would not be parties to a social compact, and the article is not as broad as the famous Massachusetts one. Another article of the Bill of Rights states, "the people shall be secure in their persons, houses, papers, and possessions from unreasonable searches and seizures"; but the usage of "people" in the United States Constitution proved, according to the court, that the word here need not include slaves. A third article in the Bill of Rights provided that "no person shall be arrested, detained, or punished, except in cases clearly warranted by law." But was this detention warranted by the law? This is to be answered by examination of the statutes; that of 1774 prohibited the importation of slaves into Connecticut, that of 1784 provided that all born "in the State" after March 1 of that year should be free at the age of twenty-five. This last law, Swift thought,[1] "has laid the foundation for the gradual abolition of slavery; for, as the children of slaves are born free, being servants only until twenty-five years of age, the consequence is that as soon as the slaves now in being shall have become extinct, slavery will cease, as the importation of slaves in future is prohibited...As slavery is gradually diminishing and will in a short time be extinguished, there being but few slaves in the State, it will be unnecessary, in this place, to make any remarks upon a subject that has so long engrossed the attention of the humane and benevolent part of mankind in the present age." These words are quoted approvingly and the statement is

---

[1] Swift's System, I., 220.

made that, unless there is some defect in the acts, there has been no real slavery in Connecticut since 1784. The acts were passed, not to interfere with vested rights, but to prevent the increase of evils which would result from the competition of slave labor "with the labor of poor whites, tending to reduce the price of their work and prevent their employment, and to bring the free laborer, in some measure, into the ranks with slaves." The Court decided that, though the law of 1774 did not prevent a master transporting a slave through the State, it did prevent him from keeping her there, and that a slave may be "left," "although the owner does not intend to reside permanently himself, or to suffer such slave permanently to remain here." On the construction of this word "left," and on the *post-nati* argument from the act of 1784, the Court declared Nancy free. As to the words "born within this State," in the act of 1784, the Court held "within this State" surplusage, stating, as a reason, that the Legislature could not legislate for any other State. At any rate it is certain that foreigners could claim no more rights than natives, and as natives can only hold persons as slaves under twenty-five years of age, citizens of other States could do no more.

The dissenting judges laid stress on the words "in this State" in the act of 1784, and claimed that "left," in the act of 1774, meant to desert, abandon, withdraw, or depart from, that mere length of stay does not matter, as long as the *animus revertendi* remains. They state, however, they are glad their interpretation does not consign the woman to slavery; though they "maintain that the State of Connecticut, from time immemorial, has been, and to a certain extent now is, a slaveholding State."

This case showed clearly that the judiciary of the State would lean to the side of freedom whenever possible, and virtually made Connecticut a free State by its liberal construction of the laws, though the formal removal of the State from the slaveholding column was not to take place for some ten years more.

THE NEGROES ON THE "AMISTAD."

In August, 1839,[1] the people of Connecticut, New York and Rhode Island were excited by tidings of a suspicious craft, thought to be a pirate. It was a long, low, black schooner, manned by negroes, and orders were issued to the United States steamer Fulton and several revenue cutters to chase her. On August 26, 1839, the United States brig Washington was sounding off Culloden Point, lying between Gardner's and Montauk Points. While there, a vessel was noticed lying off the shore and a boat passing between her and the shore, where a number of persons were with carts and horses. Lieut. Gedney, commanding the Washington, sent a boat to investigate, and when the vessel was boarded she proved to be manned by negroes, of whom about twenty were on board, together with two white men, who came forward and claimed protection.[2] The story was soon told. The vessel was a slaver, the Amistad, which had brought African slaves kidnapped in April, from Lemboko, in the Mendi country, near Liberia. Jose Ruiz bought forty-nine of them and Pedro Montes took four more. These they re-embarked on the Amistad at Havana on June 27, 1839, and sailed for Guanajah, Porto Principe. It will be remembered that the slave trade was prohibited by Spain and the Africans so introduced ought still to be free. The trade was, however, carried on surreptitiously to a large extent, and those thus taken to Cuba were called " Bozals," in distinction from the " Ladrinos,"[3] or native slaves. The ship's

---

[1] This account is chiefly drawn from Wilson, " Rise and Fall of the Slave Power," Vol. I., pp. 456-466; J. Q. Adams' Diary; Niles' Register; Williams, " Hist. of Negro Race," II., p. 93; Barber, Jno. W., "A History of the Amistad Captives...with Biographical Sketches of each of the surviving Africans, also an account of the trials had on their case, etc.," New Haven, 1840; S. E. Baldwin, " The Captives of the Amistad," N. H. Col. Hist. Papers. IV., pp. 397-404.

[2] Niles' Reg., Vol. 57, pp. 1, 28, 29.

[3] A false translation of this word in a public document caused great trouble. Niles' Reg., Vol. 59, p. 301.

papers falsely referred to them as "ladrinos," legal slaves. The captain of the ship was Ramon Ferrers, and the crew seems to have consisted of two men and a cook, besides a negro cabin-boy. On the fifth night out from Havana the slaves rose, under the leadership of Joseph Cinquez or Cingue, attacked and slew the captain and cook with knives such as were used to cut sugar-cane, and, according to one story, slew the two men in the crew. The cabin-boy, Antonio, however, said in court that the men lowered a small boat and escaped. Ruiz and Montes were bound and kept alive to navigate the ship. The negroes tried to return to Africa and had the vessel steered eastward by the sun during the day, while by night the white men steered to the northwest, hoping to fall in with a man-of-war or to reach some country. After boxing for four days in Bahamas Channel, they steered for St. Andrew Island, near New Providence; thence to Green Key, where the blacks laid in a supply of water; thence for New Providence, where the negroes would not suffer the vessel to enter port, but anchored off the coast every night. The whites were treated with some severity, and with the constant fear of death staring them in the face, their lot must have been most unenviable. Montes, too, was suffering from two wounds in the head and arm. The ship was three days off Long Island, to the eastward of New Providence, and then two months on the ocean, during which time they were boarded several times by vessels, once by an American schooner from Kingston, which remained alongside for twenty-four hours and traded with the negroes, finding they had plenty of money. This was the Spaniards' story, to which they added that they were always sent below in such cases. Our admiration for Cinquez rises when we consider that, for this long period, he managed to continue his ascendancy over his comrades, especially considering how difficult were the circumstances of the case. On August 20, near New York harbor, a pilot-boat met the Amistad and furnished the negroes apples, and when, shortly after, a second one met them, they suspected the whites had taken them to a strange land and refused to let the pilot board her, while they exhibited such anger towards the Spaniards that they feared for their lives more than ever. On the 24th, off Montauk Light, the Spaniards tried to run the vessel aground, but failed, and the tide drifted it on, until they anchored where they were found. After anchoring, about twenty of the negroes went on shore for water and three of them bought dogs from some of the inhabitants. The news quickly spread. Capt. Green, who came up, according to his report, induced the negroes to promise to give him the ship. They desired him to take them to Sierra Leone. Just then appeared Lieut. Gedney and took possession of the vessel and of the negroes. Before Cinquez would suffer himself to be taken he leapt overboard and loosed from his waist into the water 300 doubloons which he had taken from the captain. The Africans taken were forty-four in number,[1] the rest having died. Of this number, three were girls, the rest men. Cinquez, the leader, was described as about twenty-five or twenty-six years of age, five feet eight inches in height, erect in figure, well built, and very active. His countenance was unusually intelligent; he possessed uncommon decision and coolness, and a composure indicative of much courage. Lieut. Gedney took the Amistad with all on board to New London, where a judicial investigation was held on August 29, on board the Washington, before the United States District Judge A. T. Judson, whom we have already seen in the Crandall trouble. As a result of this examination the Africans were taken to the New Haven jail on Sept. 1, and on the 14th were removed to Hartford, save one left behind on account of sickness. The case now became very complicated. Ruiz and Montes claimed the Africans as their slaves and preferred charges of murder against them. The Africans claimed freedom and, through their friends, preferred charges of assault and battery and of false imprisonment against Ruiz and

---

[1] Niles' Reg., Vol. 57, p. 48 and 50. They were shown in Hartford at 12½ cents admission. Wild stories were spread that one of them was a cannibal.

Montes. Lieut. Gedney claimed salvage on vessel, cargo and slaves. Capt. Green and the Long Islanders had a counter claim for the same. The owners of the cargo in Havana claimed it, and the Spanish minister, " forgetful of his country's laws," demanded not only that it, but also that the blacks be given up under the treaty of 1795, that the negroes might be tried in Cuba, and maintained that if they should be tried, convicted and executed in Connecticut, the effect would not be as good as if done in Cuba. The District Attorney, Holabird, claimed that the Africans should be held subject to the President's orders, to be taken back to Africa, according to the Act of 1819, and that, as the Government of Spain had claimed them, they should be kept until the pleasure of the United States be known. Holabird was thoroughly subservient to the slavery interest and wrote to the Secretary of State asking if there were not treaty stipulations which would authorize " our government " to deliver them up to Spain, and if so, " whether it would be done before our court sits," as he did not wish them tried there. The Secretary of State knew there was no such treaty, and if there were, as Wilson well says, the President could not supersede criminal warrants, but he instructed the District Attorney "to take care that no proceedings of your Circuit Court, or any other judicial tribunal, place the vessel, cargo, or slaves ('a gratuitous assumption,' remarks Wilson) beyond the control of the Federal Executive." While the demands of Calderon, the Spanish minister, were supported by the pro-slavery press, the anti-slavery men in New York City appointed a committee, composed of S. S. Jocelyn, Joshua Leavitt, and Lewis Tappan, to solicit funds, employ counsel, and see that the interests of the Africans were carefully cared for. As a result, Seth P. Staples and Theodore Sedgwick, Jr., of New York, were employed as counsel and wrote to President Van Buren denying that these Africans were slaves, contending that, in rising against the whites, they only obeyed the dictates of self-defense, and praying that their case should not be decided "in the recesses of the Cabinet, where these unfriended men can have no counsel and can produce no proof; but in the halls of Justice, with the safeguards she throws around the unfriended and oppressed." The letter was turned over to Felix Grundy, the Attorney General, a violent opponent of emancipation, and one who favored surrender to Spain. He replied he could see no "legal principle upon which the government would be justified in going into an investigation for the purpose of ascertaining the facts set forth in the papers clearing the vessel from one Spanish port to another" as evidence as to whether the negroes were slaves or not. He thought, as the Africans were charged with violation of Spain's laws, they should be surrendered; so that, if guilty, "they might not escape punishment," and that, to fulfil treaty obligations, the President should issue an order, directing the marshal to deliver the vessel and cargo to such persons as Calderon should designate. This Van Buren could not do, as there was no extradition treaty with Spain, which fact Grundy ought to have known. On Sept. 17th, the United States Circuit Court met in Hartford, Judge Thompson presiding, and on the 18th a writ of Habeas Corpus was applied for by the two lawyers mentioned and Roger S. Baldwin of New Haven, in behalf of the three girls, who were only detained as witnesses. On the 21st instant, the same writ was applied for in behalf of the rest of the Africans. Judge Thompson overruled the claim of Lieut. Gedney and Capt. Green for salvage, but refused to grant habeas corpus to any, though ample security were offered, on the ground that the case would first come regularly before the District Court, and the District Court having jurisdiction is bound to provide necessaries for the Africans, until their status is determined. Mr. Staples claimed the case should be tried in New York; but the judge decided that, as the ship was taken on the high seas, i. e., beyond low water-mark, the suit should be tried where the vessel was first brought to land. He also decided the Africans should not be held for murder on the high seas.[1] On Oct. 19th, the District Court met, heard testimony, and

---

[1] Full text of decision in Niles' Reg., Vol. 57, pp. 73-75.

adjourned to meet in New Haven, Jan. 7th, 1840.[1] On Nov. 26th, 1839, De Argaiz, the new Spanish minister, wrote to the Secretary of State, denying the right of the United States courts to take cognizance of the case, and complained that through their delay, public vengeance had not been satisfied, for Spain "does not demand the delivery of slaves but of assassins." From this high moral tone, he descended in another letter to ask that, on the release of the negroes by the court, the President should order the transportation of the negroes to Cuba in a government vessel. The assurance of this request was not resented by the President. On the contrary, he ordered such a vessel to be ready to take the negroes, if released, to Cuba and deliver them to the Captain General of the island. This vessel, the Grampus, was stationed off New Haven, three days after the court assembled, ostensibly to give the negroes "opportunity to prove their freedom." Before the court even assembled, Lieuts. Gedney and Meade of the Washington were ordered to be ready to go to Cuba with the negroes at the United States' expense. "for the purpose of affording their testimony in any proceedings that may be ordered by the authorities of Cuba in the matter." This shameful pre-judgment of the case and eager desire to be subservient to the slavery interest is most disgraceful to Van Buren's administration. On Jan. 7th, 1840, the District Court met, and the counsel for the Africans offered such conclusive testimony that the negroes were native Africans and not Spanish subjects, that Judge Judson said the point was clearly proved. Gedney[2] claimed one-third of the vessel and cargo as salvage, which was given him by the Court; but his claim for salvage on the negroes was refused by the Court, as the negroes could not be sold, there being no law to permit this to be done. Green said he did not wish salvage on flesh, but, if the negroes were slaves, he wanted his share.

---
[1] Full text of proceedings in Niles' Reg., Vol. 57, pp. 222, 223.
[2] The Spanish owners unsuccessfully tried to prevent his getting salvage, on the ground that, as a United States officer, what he did was in the line of his duty and should have no pay.

The Court speedily dismissed his claim and decided that only Antonio, the cabin-boy, should be given up to Spain, and that the rest should be transported to Africa. This decision was made by a strong Democrat and a man in nowise friendly to negroes, as was shown in the Canterbury affair, and is so the more noteworthy.[1] The District Attorney, by order of the Secretary of State, appealed the case and, in his zeal, sent a messenger to Washington to have a clerical mistake in the President's warrant corrected, that the negroes might be held. In returning the warrant, Mr. Forsyth, the Secretary of State, wrote, " I have to state, by direction of the President, that if the decision of the court is such as is anticipated, the order of the President is to be carried into execution, unless an appeal shall actually have been interposed. You are not to take it for granted that it will be interposed." That is, if the counsel for the Africans did not at once appeal, these were to be hurried on the Grampus and taken to Cuba. On the very day[2] the court assembled, Van Buren sent directions to the Marshal for this purpose, and so " flagitious and barefaced was deemed this order," says Wilson, that some of Van Buren's friends said later that it was issued without his knowledge, by his " sanguine and not over-scrupulous Secretary." Justice Thompson affirmed the decision of the District Court *pro forma*, and left the whole matter to be decided by the United States Supreme Court on an appeal. The committee appointed to care for the Africans now prepared for the last appeal, without stint of time or money, and to the four[3] lawyers already employed added John Quincy Adams, with " his great learning and forensic ability, his commanding position and well-earned reputation." As early as Sept. 23d, 1839, we read in the diary of the " old man eloquent," " Mr. Francis Jackson brought me a letter from Mr. Ellis Gray Loring, requesting my opinion upon the knotty questions involved in the case of the Spanish ship

---

[1] Niles' Reg., Vol. 57, pp. 336, 352, 384.
[2] April 29, 1840, at New Haven. Niles' Reg., Vol. 58, p. 160.
[3] Mr. Kimberley made the fourth.

Amistad.... I desired Mr. J. to say that I felt some delicacy about answering his letter, until Judge Thompson's opinion shall be published and until the final decision of the Government in the whole case." Meantime he asked Jackson to look up the records. Soon after, on Oct. 1st, we read,[1] "that which now absorbs a great part of my time and all my good feelings is the case of fifty-three African negroes, taken at sea off Montauk Point by Lieut. Gedney."[2] He gives a summary of the case up to that date and, on the next day, having thrown himself into the case with all his accustomed zeal and energy, he writes that he has examined all the authorities. "Here is an enormous consumption of time, only to perplex myself with a multitude of questions upon which I cannot yet make up opinions, for which I am willing to be responsible."[3] We hear no more of the case for some time. On Feb. 10th, 1840, he offered a resolution calling upon the President[4] for papers concerning the Amistad and, on May 25th, offered a resolution denouncing the detention and imprisonment of the Africans, which was read but not received.[5] His interest in the case continued, and on Oct. 27th, Ellis Gray Loring and Lewis Tappan called on this dauntless advocate of the right of petition and entreated him[6] to act as assistant counsel for the Africans at the January term of the Supreme Court. He writes: "I endeavored to excuse myself upon the plea of my age and inefficiency, of the excessive burden of my duties.... But they urged me so much and represented the case of those unfortunate men as so critical, it being a case of life and death, that I yielded and told them that, if by the blessing of God my health and strength should permit, I would argue the case before the Supreme Court, and I implore the mercy of Almighty God so to control my temper, to enlighten my soul, and to give me utterance, that I may prove myself in every respect equal to the task."[7]

---

[1] Diary, X., 132. [2] Diary, X., 133. [3] Diary, X., 135.
[4] Diary, X., 215. Niles' Reg., Vol. 58, p. 59.
[5] Diary, X., 296. [6] Diary, X., 358.
[7] Diary, X., 360. Niles' Reg., Vol. 57, pp. 99, 105, 176.

A month later, Nov. 17th, he visited Gov. Baldwin in New Haven and saw the prisoners, thirty-six of whom were confined in one chamber, in size about 30 by 20 feet. All but one of the men seemed under thirty. Three of them tried to read to him from the New Testament, and one wrote a tolerable hand. The chiefs, Cinquez and Grabow, had remarkable countenances, he thought. The people of New Haven, and especially the students in the Yale Divinity School, did not neglect the temporal or spiritual interests of the captives; they fed and clothed them, studied their language, taught them to read and write, and instructed them in the truths of Christianity.

During the following months[1] Mr. Adams busily prepared for the case, being assisted by Mr. Stephen Fox, the British minister. On Feb. 22d, the Amistad case came up before the august tribunal. On that day, Attorney-General Henry D. Gilpin spoke for the government and Gov. Baldwin for the captives, in a "sound and eloquent, but exceedingly mild and moderate argument,"[2] which he continued on the next day.

On the 24th, John Quincy Adams rose[3] to speak before an audience that filled, but did not crowd, the court-room, and in which he remarked there were not many ladies. He wrote in his diary: "I had been deeply distressed and agitated till the moment when I rose, and then my spirit did not sink within me. With grateful heart for aid from above, though in humiliation for the weakness incident to the limits of my powers, I spoke for four hours and a half...The structure of my argument...is perfectly simple and comprehensive...admitting the steady and undeviating pursuit of one fundamental principle." Against him "an immense array of power—the Executive Administration, instigated by the minister of a foreign nation, has been brought to bear in

---

[1] Diary, X., 396, 399, 401. Niles' Reg., Vol. 57, p. 417, Vol. 58, p. 3. Calhoun animadverts on British interference on March 13, 1840. Niles' Reg., Vol. 58, p. 140.
[2] Diary, X., 429.   [3] Diary, X., 431.

this case on the side of injustice.... I did not, I could not answer public expectation; but I have not yet utterly failed. God speed me to the end." On the 25th, he spoke for four and a half hours more, and on March 1st, the Court having meantime been in adjournment on account of the sudden death of Mr. Justice Barbour, he spoke four hours more and finished his argument. On the next day Mr. Gilpin closed the case for the United States. Mr. Adams, in his argument, sternly condemned the National Government from the President down.[1] He maintained that these Africans were torn from home and shipped against the laws of the United States and the laws of nations, that their passage on the Amistad was in law and fact a continuance of the original voyage, and that sixteen of the number had perished through the cruelty of Ruiz and Montes, on whose souls the ghosts of these slain must sit heavy through the closing hours of life. He animadverted severely on the conduct of the Secretary of State, saying that he ought instantly to have answered the Spanish minister that his demands were inadmissible and that the President had no power to do what was requested. He should have said that he could not deliver up the ship to the owner, for he was dead; that the question depended upon the courts; that a declaration to the President that the courts had no power to try the case involved an offensive demand, and that the delivering the negroes by the President and sending them beyond the seas for trial was making the President "a constable, a catchpole." The Secretary of State had not asserted the rights of the nation against these extraordinary demands. "He has degraded the country in the face of the civilized world, not only by allowing these demands to remain unanswered, but by proceeding, I am obliged to say, throughout the whole transaction, as if the Executive were earnestly desirous to comply with every one of these demands." He said the Spanish minister persisted in his requests because "he was not told instantly, without the delay of an hour, that this government could never admit

---

[1] Diary, X., 435.

such claims, and would be offended if they were repeated, or any portion of them. Yet all these claims, monstrous, absurd, and inadmissible as they are, have been urged and repeated for eighteen months on our government, and an American Secretary of State evades answering them—evades it to such an extent that the Spanish minister reproaches him for not answering his arguments." In his scathing and relentless manner he next proceeded to attack Grundy's order, mentioned previously, and asking why it was not acted upon, he cried out, " Why did not the President send an order at once to the marshal to seize these men and ship them beyond the seas, or deliver them to the Spanish minister? I am ashamed—I am ashamed of my country, that such an opinion should have been delivered by any public officer, especially by the legal counsellor of the Executive. I am ashamed to stand up before the nations of the earth with such an opinion recorded before us as official, and still more, adopted by a Cabinet which did not dare to do the deed." Such is a brief outline of his forcible address.

A week later, March 9, Justice Story gave the opinion of the court[1] that the Africans were kidnapped and unlawfully transported to Cuba, purchased by Ruiz and Montes with knowledge of the fact that they were free, and did not become pirates and robbers in taking the Amistad and trying to regain their country; that there was nothing in the treaty with Spain which justified a surrender, and that the United States had to respect the Africans' rights as much as those of the Spaniards. " Our opinion is that the decree of the Circuit Court affirming that of the District Court ought to be affirmed, except so far as it directs the negroes to be delivered to the President to be transported to Africa, in pursuance of the Act of the 3d of March, 1819, and as to this it ought to be reversed, and that the said negroes be declared to be free and be dismissed from the custody of the court and go with-

---

[1] Text of decision in Niles' Reg., Vol. 60, p. 40 ff., vide Vol. 60, p. 32. The influence of Great Britain was continuously thrown on the side of freedom. Niles' Reg., Vol. 59, p. 402.

out day." The battle was won. John Quincy Adams[1] wrote to Lewis Tappan, "The captives are free. The part of the decree of the District Court which placed them at the disposal of the President of the United States to be sent to Africa, is removed. They are to be discharged from the custody of the marshal, free."

A week later,[2] on March 17, Mr. Adams asked Webster, the new Secretary of State, for a public ship to take the Africans home, as the court had taken from them "the vessel found in their possession...and her cargo, their lawful prize of war." Webster, Adams writes in his diary, appeared startled at the idea that the Amistad and her cargo were the property of the Africans, but afterwards said he saw no objection to furnish them with a passage in a public ship and would speak of it to the Secretary of the Navy. He, however, finally refused to grant the request.[3]

Lewis Tappan had been largely instrumental in their release. He left his business and traveled for weeks in their behalf, counseling with friends, getting money, and making arrangements to send them to Africa. He exhibited them throughout the North for an admission fee to raise money for their passage. After their release,[4] they were sent to Farmington, Connecticut, for instruction, and many of them learned to speak English and became Christians. Religious people throughout the country became interested in them, and when they went back to Africa on November 25, 1841, five missionaries went with the thirty-five that survived.[5] They landed at Sierra Leone on January 15, 1842, whence the

---

[1] Adams wrote on March 17, 1841, strenuously opposing many of the incidental positions taken by the lower courts. Text in full in Niles' Reg., Vol. 60, p. 116.

[2] Diary, X., 446. The vessel was sold at New London in October, 1840. The cargo was also sold, the whole bringing about $6000. Niles' Reg., Vol. 59, pp. 144, 318, 347.

[3] Niles' Reg., Vol. 62, p. 144.

[4] Diary, X., 450. Niles' Reg., Vol. 60, p. 64; Vol. 62, pp. 17, 128, 311.

[5] Niles' Reg., Vol. 62, pp. 96, 224.

British Government assisted them home, and from this band of negroes in the Amistad sprung the Mendi Mission.[1]

In 1844, C. J. Ingersoll,[2] Chairman of the Committee of Foreign Affairs of the House of Representatives, reported a bill to pay $70,000 to the pretended owners of the Africans; but the burning words of Giddings and Adams secured the passage of a motion to lay on the table and prevented that national disgrace. As late as 1847, however, Polk, in his message, recommended an appropriation to the Spanish Government to be distributed among the claimants.[3]

Of the fifty-three Africans on the Amistad when it left Cuba, nine died on the way, eight at New Haven, and one at Farmington, while Cinque and thirty-four others lived to return home.[4]

Growth of the Anti-Slavery Spirit.

The coming of the Revolution caused men to question the rightfulness of holding one's fellow-man in bondage, and the article in the *Norwich Packet* and the resolutions of the Danbury town meeting, already quoted, clearly show this. The feeling spread. In 1778, the Wethersfield town records show a slave, Prince, manumitted, on his master's " being convinced[5] of the injustice of the general practice of the country in holding negro slaves, during life, without their consent."

Many other such instances are doubtless hidden away in the manuscripts of the Town Clerks' offices, but the only other one I have come across is that of Abijah Holbrook,

---

[1] On February 27, 1843, President Tyler recommended Congress, by a special message, to refund the salvage on the Amistad to the Spanish Government. Niles' Reg., Vol. 64, p. 66.

[2] Adams issued an address to his constituents on this subject concerning this. The text is in Niles' Reg., Vol. 68, p. 85.

[3] Niles' Reg., Vol. 73, Dec. 11, 1847.

[4] Niles' Reg., Vol. 60, pp. 206, 208, 400. The cabin-boy Antonio was to have been returned to Cuba, but escaped. Niles' Reg., Vol. 60, p. 96.

[5] Mag. of Am. Hist., XXI., 422.

who came from Massachusetts to Torrington in 1787, and in 1798 freed his slave, "then about 28 years old" and "desirous of being free,...being influenced by motives of humanity and benevolence, believing that all mankind by nature are entitled to equal liberty and freedom." His negroes, he said, "have served me with faithfulness and fidelity, and they being now in the prime and vigor of life, and appear to be well qualified, as to understanding and economy, to maintain and support themselves by their own industry, and they manifesting a great desire to be delivered from slavery and bondage,"[1] he grants their desire. Before that, however, an organized anti-slavery sentiment had arisen. In February, 1789, the Rhode Island[2] Anti-Slavery Society was founded, with Jonathan Edwards the younger, pastor of a New Haven church, as one of the members. In Connecticut there were less than 3000 slaves, yet "the strong pro-slavery feeling and conservative interest which obtained there opened a wide and important field for an Abolition Society." So, in 1790, the Connecticut Anti-Slavery Society[3] was formed, with President Ezra Stiles, of Yale College, as its president, and Simeon Baldwin as its secretary.

The Society speedily showed great activity. On January 7, 1791, it issued a petition[4] to Congress, which was referred to a special committee and never more heard of.

In the petition,[5] the Society, though "lately established," claims it has "become generally extensive through the State, and we fully believe embraces on this subject the sentiments of a large majority of the citizens. From a sober conviction of the unrighteousness of slavery, your petitioners have long beheld with grief a considerable number of our fellow-men

---

[1] Orcutt's "Hist. of Torrington," p. 212.
[2] Wilson, "Rise and Fall," I., p. 26.
[3] Poole, "Anti-Slavery Opinions before 1800," p. 50.
[4] Presented to Congress, Dec. 8, 1791. Wilson, "Rise and Fall," I., p. 67.
[5] Found in "Memorials presented to Congress by Different Societies instituted for promoting the Abolition of Slavery." Phila., 1792, pp. 7-11.

doomed to perpetual bondage, in a country which boasts of her freedom...The whole system of African slavery is unjust in its nature, impolitic in its principles, and in its consequences ruinous to the industry and enterprise of the citizens of these States." They pray that Congress should, by constitutional means, "prevent, as much as possible, the horrors of the slave-trade,...prohibit the citizens of the United States from carrying on the trade,...prohibit foreigners from fitting out vessels...in the United States for transporting persons from Africa,...and alleviate the sufferings of those who are now in slavery, and check the further progress of this inhuman commerce."

The same year[1] in which this temperate appeal was written, Jonathan Edwards, Jr., speaking before the Connecticut Society, said, " Every man who cannot show that his negro hath by his voluntary conduct forfeited his liberty, is obliged immediately to manumit him." " To hold a man in a state of slavery who has a right to his liberty, is to be every day guilty of robbing him of his liberty, or of man-stealing, and is a greater sin in the sight of God than concubinage or fornication." In these trenchant words, as Wilson truly remarks,[2] " was clearly promulgated the duty of immediate emancipation, as distinctly as it has ever been enunciated... before or since."

Though not so extreme as this, when a proposition for a duty on slaves was before the Congress of the United States, at about the same time, Roger Sherman objected to this being included in the general import bill, saying,[3] " He could not reconcile himself to the insertion of human beings as a subject of import, among goods, wares, and merchandise." On this same subject, some years later, Roger Griswold spoke

---

[1] " Injustice and Impolicy of the Slave Trade and of the Slavery of the Africans, Illustrated in a sermon before the Connecticut Society for the promotion of freedom and for the relief of persons unlawfully holden in Bondage, at their annual meeting." By Jonathan Edwards, D. D., New Haven, Sept. 15, 1791.

[2] Wilson, " Rise and Fall," I., 27.

[3] Wilson, " Rise and Fall," I., p. 56.

against laying a tax on imported slaves,[1] though he was opposed to the slave-trade, lest it should seem the United States raised money from commerce in slaves. The mass of the citizens of Connecticut at this time were evidently abolitionists of a moderate type, believing, as did the Fathers of the Republic, that emancipation would come gradually. Meantime the movement towards liberty was growing, and when the Anti-Slavery Societies became strong enough to hold their first Convention at Philadelphia, on January 1, 1794, the Connecticut Society was represented by Uriah Tracy. On the 8th of May of the same year,[2] the day of the inauguration of the Governor, the Society was entertained by an address at the North (now Centre) Meeting House, delivered by Theodore Dwight, its secretary. His address was published, and it was probably from having seen or heard of it that Bishop Gregoire mentioned Dwight in the list of fifteen to whom he dedicated his "Literature of Negroes." In this list, it may be remarked, were the names of two other Connecticut men: Joel Barlow and Col. Humphreys.

At the time of Dwight's address, there were Committees of Correspondence at Hartford,[3] and in New London, Windham and Tolland Counties. When the second Anti-Slavery Convention met at Philadelphia in 1795, Connecticut was represented by Jonathan Edwards, Uriah Tracy, and Zephaniah Swift. The first of these was made chairman of the committee on business, and prepared an address to South Carolina,[4] appealing for "a numerous class of men, existing among

---

[1] In 1804. Wilson, "Rise and Fall," I., p. 87.
[2] Poole, "Anti-Slavery Opinions before 1800," pp. 50, 80. "Oration Spoken before the Conn. Society for the Promotion of Freedom and the Relief of Persons unlawfully Held in Bondage, Convened at Hartford on the 8th Day of May, 1794, by Theodore Dwight." Hartford, 1794, pp. 24, 8vo. At that time Chauncey Goodrich was vice-president and Ezekiel Williams assistant secretary.
[3] At Hartford the Committee consisted of Dr. Lemuel Hopkins, Theodore Dwight, Thomas Y. Seymour, and Ezekiel Williams, Jr. Trumbull's "Memorial Hist. of Hartford Co.," Vol. I.
[4] Poole, "Anti-Slavery Opinions," pp. 28, 77.

you, deprived of their natural rights and forcibly held in bondage." He called on the State to improve their condition and to educate them, and stated that by the slave-trade, of necessity, "the minds of our citizens are debased and their hearts hardened, by contemplating these people only through the medium of avarice or prejudice."

The early anti-slavery feeling,[1] however, gradually died away in Connecticut, as elsewhere, and was succeeded by the colonization idea, as advanced by the American Colonization Society, of which Dr. Leonard Bacon wrote, "It is not a missionary society, nor a society for the suppression of the slave-trade, nor a society for the improvement of the blacks, nor a society for the abolition of slavery; it is simply a society for the establishment of a colony on the coast of Africa." In the same line of thought, the New Haven *Religious Intelligencer* condemned measures calculated to bind the colored people to this country, by seeking to raise them to a level with the whites, whether by founding colleges or in any other way, "because it would divert attention and counteract and thwart the whole plan of colonization." It was this same spirit that aroused the opposition to Miss Crandall, and which opposed the attempt of a convention of free colored people in Philadelphia in 1831 to establish a collegiate school on the manual labor plan at New Haven. The idea of this convention was to raise $20,000 for this school, of which they stated $1000 was already offered, provided the rest should be subscribed. The reasons for their selecting New Haven were these: the site of the town was healthy and beautiful; the inhabitants friendly, pious, generous, and humane; the laws of Connecticut salutary and protected all without regard to complexion; the boarding there was cheap and the provisions good; the situation was as central as any that could be obtained with the same advantages; the extensive West India trade of New Haven might induce many wealthy colored inhabitants of the West Indies to send their

---

[1] Wilson, "Rise and Fall," I., p. 215.

sons there for an education; and lastly, the literary and scientific character of New Haven renders it a desirable place to locate their college.[1]

The plan was not looked upon with any pleasure in New Haven, and " created the most profound excitement and called forth the most determined resistance." The Mayor called a public meeting " to take into consideration a scheme said to be in progress for the establishment in this city of a college for the education of colored youth." At the meeting held September 8, 1831, resolutions were passed " that we will resist the establishment of the proposed college in this place by every lawful means," and, in the preamble, the citizens expressed their conviction that immediate emancipation and the founding of colleges for colored persons were unwarrantable and dangerous interference with the internal concerns of the State, which ought to be discouraged. To these sentiments only one man, the Rev. Simeon S. Jocelyn, entered a protest. This opposition of the residents of New Haven rendered any attempt to carry out the convention's scheme futile. The party of the *status quo ante* was triumphant throughout the State; but, as often when the hour is the darkest, the daylight was at hand.

However, there had never been lack of men to protest against human slavery, and the halls of Congress had often heard bold sentiments from Connecticut men. In November, 1797, when the Pennsylvania Quakers complained to Congress that slaves emancipated by Friends in North Carolina had again been made slaves, Allen of Connecticut said he trusted the petition would not be rejected, as that would be disrespectful to a society revered by every man who sets value on virtue. In December, 1799, when the Southerners were raging on account of a petition from the negroes of Philadelphia for gradual emancipation, Edmond of Connecticut said they were acting with " inattention that passion alone could dictate." In the session of 1806-7, when South-

---

[1] Williams. " Negro Race," II., pp. 63. 64. Fowler. " Hist. Status." p. 151.

erners sneered at the North's opposition to the slave-trade, Moseley of Connecticut said if any of his section were convicted of being in the slave trade, his constituents would thank the South for hanging them.[1] In January, 1818, when a bill to enforce the fugitive slave law was under debate, Williams of Connecticut opposed a clause permitting freemen to be dragged to another part of the country, saying, " In attempting to guard the rights of property to one class of citizens, it was unjust that the rights of another class should be put in jeopardy."

In 1833, however, the influence of those in favor of immediate abolition of slavery began to be felt in Connecticut, contending with the pro-slavery and colonization influences. In that year, the New Haven Anti-Slavery Society was founded, being one of the first societies[2] based on the principle of immediate, unconditional abolition. It sent its greetings to the old Pennsylvania Abolition Society, and received from it a cordial response. Among the leading spirits of the Connecticut Society were two clergymen,[3] Samuel J. May and Simeon S. Jocelyn, both of whom were prominent at the organization of the American Anti-Slavery Society in December, 1833.

The feeling of the learned and powerful city of New Haven was further shown in the public meeting called by the Mayor and Council of the city to consider the report and resolutions of Charleston, S. C., held August 10, 1835, and sent to each incorporated city and town in the United States. Charleston's resolves were concerning " societies and individuals who have circulated incendiary publications through some of the Southern States," and were violently against anti-slavery publications. Henry S. Edwards acted as president of the New Haven meeting, and Noah Webster and David Daggett as vice-presidents. It passed resolutions condemning abolitionist publications, denouncing their being sent by mail,

---

[1] Wilson, " Rise and Fall," I., pp. 73, 77, 82, 96.
[2] Wilson, " Rise and Fall," I., p. 25.
[3] May was Vice-President. Wilson, " Rise and Fall," I., 250 and 260.

quoting a report of a committee of Congress in 1790 that that body " have no authority to interfere in the emancipation of slaves, or in the treatment of them in the different States, it remaining with the several States alone to provide any regulations therein which humane and true policy may require." To this utterance of non-interference, they coupled another quotation from a letter of Oliver Wolcott, Sr., to his son of the same name. "I wish that Congress would prefer the white people of this country to the black. After they have taken care of the former, they may amuse themselves with the other people."[1]

Hartford held a similar meeting on Sept. 26, 1835, and, with Isaac Toucey as president and Elisha Phelps and Joseph Platt as vice-presidents, affirmed that " certain persons in the Middle and Eastern States have formed associations for the avowed purpose of effecting the abolition of slavery in the other States, and in pursuance of said design, have established a press from which they issued several newspapers and periodicals devoted to the aforesaid objects and filled with the most inflammatory matter, whereby the confederacy is endangered."

In that same year a negro woman,[2] who had fled from her master and lived in Hartford as a servant for several years, met a nephew of her former master on the streets of the city. He spoke kindly to her and told her his family had ceased to count her as their property, and that he had only friendly feelings for her. He continued that he had some clothing for her at the hotel where he was stopping, which he asked her to

---

[1] Another resolution favored colonization in Africa. Fowler, " Local Law," pp. 96, 97. Full text in Niles' Reg., Vol. 49, p. 73. R. S. Baldwin opposed these resolutions. On the same page in Niles' Reg. is a letter copied from the Middletown *Advocate*, and written by Rev. Wilbur Fisk, first President of Wesleyan University, stating that though he wished " freedom to the slave," he would sign no petitions for abolition of slavery, as " the ultra-abolitionists, by their imprudent movements and ill-timed and ill-managed system of agitation have, as I think, removed all hope of success in any measure of this kind at the present time."
[2] Trumbull's " Hartford County," I., 609.

go with him and get. She incautiously went to his room on the third floor, when he locked the door to hold her prisoner. She rushed to the front window and leapt out, and, falling on an awning, escaped alive. Mr. Elisha Colt, in whose family she served, raised a purse and bought her, that he might set her free.

Another fugitive slave in Hartford was Rev. James Pennington, D. D., who, escaping when a boy, was educated abroad at Heidelberg. He became pastor of the Talcott St. Church in Hartford, and being fearful of capture after the passage of the fugitive slave law of 1850, induced Gen. Joseph R. Hawley, then a young lawyer in the office of John Hooker, Esq., to visit his former owner and buy him for Mr. Hooker. Mr. Hooker held the deed for a day, to enjoy the sensation of owning a doctor of divinity, and then emancipated him.

In 1836[1] the Connecticut Society, urged on by the Crandall case, started the *Christian Freeman* at Hartford, with Wm. H. Burleigh as editor. In 1845, that paper was merged in the *Charter Oak*, whose office was mobbed by a Democratic mob during the Mexican War, on account of the outspoken character of its sentiments. The *Charter Oak* was merged in the *Republican* in later years, that in the *Evening Press*, and that in the well known *Hartford Courant*.[2]

Under the stimulus of the zeal of the leaders of this new movement, violent discussion and debate sprang up throughout the State.[3] Amos A. Phelps, a brilliant and able speaker, a native of Farmington, took the matter up in that town, and the church in the town was nearly rent in twain from the violence of the parties.[4] What nearly happened in Farmington came to pass in Guilford, where the pastor

---

[1] The increased interest in the subject is shown by the number of pamphlets issued upon slavery in Connecticut about this time.
[2] Trumbull's "Hartford County," I., p. 609.
[3] Niles' Reg., Vol. 56, p. 410, has a long letter from Roger M. Sherman, dated June 26, 1838, written to the National Anti-Slavery Society, in which, in dignified language, he states his opposition both to slavery and the methods of the abolitionists.
[4] Trumbull's "Hartford County," II., p. 192.

changed from the advocacy of colonization to that of abolition, and caused such a bitter dissension that, though he eventually resigned and left the town, his followers, who constituted a minority in the old church, left and established another one, which remains separate to this day. In that town the use of the church was refused the local Anti-Slavery Society for its meetings, and in Norwich, which, on Oct. 14, 1800, had directed its selectmen to instruct the town's representatives "to use their influence in obtaining a resolve... prohibiting the migration of negroes...from other States into this State," now the inhabitants in town meeting "Resolved that, as it is the duty of every good citizen to discountenance seditious or incendiary doctrines of every sort, we do deny entirely the use of the Town Hall, or of any other building belonging to the town, for any purpose connected in any way with the abolition of slavery."[1]

Miss Abbey Kelley,[2] a Quakeress, who spoke against slavery, was denounced from the pulpits in Litchfield County as "that woman Jezebel, who calleth herself a prophetess to teach and seduce my servants"; but she and others gathered so many adherents that in January, 1837, a meeting was held at Wolcottville to organize an anti-slavery society. The gathering had to be in a barn, as churches and other public places were closed. Even there a mob broke up the meeting, which adjourned to Torrington Church, where it continued two days. The Litchfield County Sociey[3] so formed soon began holding monthly meetings in barns, sheds, and groves, and propagating its tenets by lectures, tracts, etc.

---

[1] Caulkins, "Norwich," p. 568.
[2] Orcutt's "Torrington," pp. 212, 218. For the opposition an early anti-slavery advocate received in Washington, Litchfield County, see "The Master of the Gunnery," a memorial volume to F. W. Gunn.
[3] Roger S. Mills of New Hartford was made president, Erastus Lyman of Goshen vice-president, with Gen. Daniel B. Brinsmade of Washington, Gen. Uriel Tuttle of Torringford, and Jonathan Coe of Winsted. Rev. R. M. Chipman of Harwinton was made secretary, and Dr. E. D. Hudson of Torringford treasurer. Torrington was the birthplace of John Brown of Ossawattomie and Harper's Ferry fame.

From 1840 onward, the progress of anti-slavery sentiments in Connecticut was gradual.¹ In 1840 she cast 174 votes for Birney; in 1844 she gave him 1943; in 1848 Van Buren received 5005; in 1852 Hale obtained 3160. Then under the influence of the Kansas-Nebraska Bill the State rapidly moved towards abolitionism. In 1854 the Anti-Nebraska candidate for Governor polled 19,465 votes; in 1856 Fremont carried the State and received 42,715 votes, and Connecticut was placed in the ranks of the Republican States for many years.

SOCIAL CONDITION OF SLAVES.

The slave showed the usual imitation of his white masters. We read of negro balls, negro governors, and negro training days. In religious affairs they, for the most part, were of the Congregational faith; few became Baptists or Methodists, as at the South. The annual election of a negro Governor² was a great event, and one, as far as I know, unique to Connecticut. It occurred as recently as 1820, and came off generally on the Saturday after election day. It was participated in by all the negroes in the capital, and not only a governor, but also minor officers were chosen. They borrowed their masters' horses and trappings and had a grand parade after the election. "Provisions, decorations, fruits, and liquors were liberally" given them. "Great electioneering prevailed, parties often ran high, stump harangues were made, and a vast deal of ceremony expended in counting the votes, proclaiming the result, and inducting the candidate into office, the whole too often terminating in a drunken frolic, if not a free fight," says one writer. Scaeva, in his "Sketches of Hartford in the Olden Time," adds other

---

¹ On Dec. 26, 1843, J. Q. Adams notes in his Diary that he presented a petition from Connecticut for the abolition of slavery and the slave trade in the District of Columbia. Diary, XI., 461. In 1845 the Abolition or Liberty nominated full State and Congressional tickets. Niles' Reg., Vol. 68. p. 23. 1841 is the earliest year in which I find an Abolition State ticket. Niles, Reg., Vol. 62. p. 80.
² Caulkins, "Norwich," pp. 330. Stiles, "Windsor," I., 490.

touches. The negroes, " of course, made their election to a large extent deputatively, as all could not be present, but uniformly yielded to it their assent.... The person they selected for the office was usually one of much note among themselves, of imposing presence, strength, firmness, and volubility, who was quick to decide, ready to command, and able to flog. If he was inclined to be arbitrary, belonged to a master of distinction, and was ready to pay freely for diversions—these were circumstances in his favor. Still it was necessary he should be an honest negro, and be, or appear to be, wise above his fellows." What his powers were was probably not well defined, but he most likely " settled all grave disputes in the last resort, questioned conduct, and imposed penalties and punishments sometimes for vice and misconduct." Such an officer is a remarkable instance of the negro's power of mimicry. In his election parade " a troop of blacks, sometimes one hundred in number, marching sometimes two and two on foot, sometimes mounted in true military style and dress on horseback, escorted him through the streets with drums beating, colors flying, and fifes, fiddles, clarionets, and every ' sonorous metal ' that could be found, ' uttering martial sound.' After marching to their content, they would retire to some large room, which they would engage for the purpose of refreshments and deliberation."

In Norwich,[1] it would seem there was a special Governor for the negroes; for the graveyard contains a stone: " In memory of Boston Trowtrow, Governor of the African tribe in this Town, who died 1772." After him ruled Sam Huntingdon, slave of the Governor of the same name, and he is described as, " after his election, riding through the Town on one of his master's horses, adorned with painted gear, his aids on each side, *à la militaire*, himself puffing and swelling with pomposity, sitting bolt upright and moving with a slow majestic pace, as if the universe was looking on. When he mounted or dismounted his aids flew to his assistance, hold-

---

[1] Caulkins, " Norwich," p. 330. *Vide* Fowler, " Hist. Status," p. 81.

ing his bridle, putting his feet into the stirrup, and bowing to the ground before him. The Great Mogul in a triumphal procession never assumed an air of more perfect self-importance than the negro Governor."

Of negro trainings, Stiles in his "Ancient Windsor" tells amusing tales, and doubtless such occurred in many other towns where there were sufficient blacks.

The Connecticut negroes, when freed, often left the State, and we have record that, when Massachusetts passed an act on March 26, 1788, that "Africans, not subjects of Morocco or citizens of one of the United States, are to be sent out of the State," there were found nine negroes and twelve mulattoes from Connecticut, though apparently not citizens of that State, as they were ordered to leave Massachusetts by a given day.[1] We hear but little of fugitive slaves. Occasionally we come across advertisements in the old Connecticut papers for runaways, but these are but few and disappear as the years pass by.[2] Generally slaves were "most tenderly cared for" in the families of their masters until death, and were sold but seldom.[3] Emancipations, beginning to be common just before the Revolution, increased more as time went on, and we frequently find applications on record to the selectmen to free the masters from responsibility in case of emancipating slaves.

It is said that at Torrington, when three men, joint owners of a female slave, in her old age hired her out to be cared for by a colored man, some indignation was raised.

When emancipated, it is noticeable that the negroes, with their gregarious tendencies, left the country places and congregated in the larger towns.[4] For example, in Suffield, where slaves were found as early as 1672, when Harry and Roco, Major Pynchon's negroes, helped build the first saw-

---

[1] Moore, "Notes on Slavery in Mass.," pp. 232-235.
[2] *Vide* Mag. of Am. Hist., XV., 614.
[3] Mag. of Am. Hist., XV., 614. N. H. Gazette, 1787.
[4] Mag. of Am. Hist., XXI., 422. Caulkins, "Norwich," p. 330. Trumbull's "Hartford County," II., p. 199.

mill, and where before 1740 there were but few slaves, mostly owned by magistrates, parsons, and tavern-keepers, the number of negroes was twenty-four in 1756; thirty-seven in 1774; fifty-three in 1782; twenty-eight in 1790; four in 1800. The last of these was manumitted in 1812, and after a few years none were left in the town. They had been a social, happy race, some of whom had married there, and all of whom had been well cared for by their masters,[1] but when freed they all drifted away to the cities, where they could have the society of others of their race. In the cities, special effort was made for the spiritual welfare of the negroes. In 1815[2] the Second Church of Norwich, under the leadership of Chas. F. Harrington, began a Sunday School for blacks, and later the Yale students in New Haven took up the same work in the Temple Street and Dixwell Avenue Schools, the latter of which is still maintained.

In general, Connecticut has little to be ashamed of in her treatment of the negroes. She treated them kindly as slaves and freed them gradually, thus avoiding any violent convulsion. Though opposed to abolitionism and interference with slavery in another State, until the aggressive character of the slaveholding power was clearly manifested, she then swung into line with the rest of the Northern States to do away with it from the soil of the whole country.

There is a steady and progressive development of the conduct of the State towards slavery. Beginning with a survival of the idea that captives in war were slaves, as shown in the conduct towards the Pequods, Connecticut acquiesced thoroughly in the principles of slavery through all the Colonial period. Her treatment of the slaves was almost always kind and generous. A master, in true patriarchal style, regarded them as in truth a part of his family.[3] With the coming of the

---

[1] Trumbull's "Hartford County," II., p. 406. Fowler, "Hist. Status," p. 149, says in Durham in 1774 there were 44 negroes, in 1868 only 3.

[2] Caulkins, "Norwich," p. 556. Fowler, "Hist. Status," p. 150, speaks of eight negro churches in the State in 1873.

[3] Fowler, "Hist. Status," pp. 81-83, gives many interesting instances of this.

Revolution and the struggle of the Colonists for freedom, a feeling arose that it was not just to hold other men in bondage, and as a result, importation of slaves was forbidden in 1774. Negroes were allowed to fight side by side with the whites, and gradual emancipation was begun in 1784. The claims of the masters were, however, respected by saving their right to those they then held as slaves, and though manumission was encouraged, the law put wise restrictions on the cruelty which would employ a man's best years in labor for another and leave him to be supported by public alms at last.

The case of Miss Prudence Crandall and of the Amistad proved effective reinforcements to the arguments of the Abolitionists, and the case of Jackson versus Bulloch showed that the courts were inclined towards the support of liberal interpretations of the anti-slavery laws. So when the formal abolition of slavery came in 1848, it found few to be affected by its provisions. The movement against slavery went on. From abolishing slavery within its borders, the State went on to forbid the seizure of a slave on its soil, and then gladly joined with the other Northern States in the great struggle which ended in the destruction of slavery throughout the United States.[1]

---

[1] In 1865, the question of negro suffrage was submitted to the voters and decided adversely by a vote of 27.217 to 33.489. In May, 1869, the legislature, by a party vote, adopted the Fifteenth Amendment to the United States Constitution. The vote in the Senate stood 12 to 5, in the House 126 to 104. Fowler. p. 266.

APPENDIX.

In addition to the works quoted in the body of the monograph, the following may be mentioned as a part of the bibliography of this subject:

Bacon, Leonard. "Slavery discussed in Occasional Essays from 1833 to 1846." New York, 1846.

Beecher, Catharine E. "An Essay on Slavery and Abolitionism." Philadelphia, 1837.

Bowne, Rev. George. "Picture of Slavery in the United States." Middletown, 1834.

Dickinson, James T. "Sermon delivered in the Second Congregational Church, Norwich, July 4, 1834, at the Request of the Anti-Slavery Society of Norwich and Vicinity." Norwich, 1834.

Fisk, Wilbur. "Substance of an Address delivered before the Middletown Colonization Society at the Annual Meeting, July 4, 1835." Middletown, 1835.

Porter, Jacob, translator. "The Well-spent Sou, or Bibles for the Poor Negro." New Haven, 1830.

Stuart, Charles. "The West India Question, reprinted from the English Quarterly Magazine and Review of April, 1832." New Haven, 1833.

Tyler, E. R. "Slaveholding a Malum in Se or Incurably Sinful." (2 editions.) Hartford, 1839.

"Fruits of Colonization—the Canterbury Persecution." 1833.

May, Samuel J. "The Right of Colored People to Education vindicated—Letters to Andrew T. Judson, Esq., and others in Canterbury, relative to Miss Crandall and her School for Colored Females." 1833.

Van Buren, Martin. Message, 1840 (Amistad).

Baldwin, Roger S., and *Adams, John Q.* "Arguments before the United States Supreme Court in the Case of the African, Cinquez or Jinque."

SLAVES AND FREE NEGROES IN CONNECTICUT.

	Slaves.	Free Negroes.
1680,	30, (Answers to Board of Trade),	...
1715,	1,500, (Niles' Register, vol. 68, p. 310),	...
1730,	700, (Answers to Board of Trade),	...
1756,	3,634, (Fowler, "Hist. Status," p. 150),	...
1762,	4,590, (Stiles MSS.),	...
1774,	6,562, (Fowler, "Hist. Status," p. 150),	...
1782,	6,281, " " "	...
1790,	2,759, (U. S. Census),	2,801
1800,	951, "	5,330
1810,	310, "	6,453
1820,	97, "	7,844
1830,	25, "	8,047
1840,	17, "	8,105
1850,	... "	7,693
1860,	... "	8,627
1870,	... "	9,668
1880,	... "	11,547
1890,	... "	12,302

N. B. Negroes on the Amistad not counted in 1840.

www.ingramcontent.com/pod-product-compliance
Lightning Source LLC
Chambersburg PA
CBHW020324090426
42735CB00009B/1401